Dead to Sin, Alive to God

Dead to Sin, Alive to God

Discover the *Power of Reckoning*
to Set You Free in Christ

Stuart C. Smith

RESOURCE *Publications* · Eugene, Oregon

Resource Publications
An Imprint of Wipf and Stock Publishers
199 W. 8th Ave., Suite 3
Eugene, OR 97401

www.wipfandstock.com

PAPERBACK ISBN: 978-1-4982-8889-7
HARDCOVER ISBN: 978-1-4982-8891-0

Manufactured in the U.S.A.

To

Christine
A model of loyal love going on 41 years

&

Clate Risley
(1915–1974)
A caring mentor when I needed hope and deliverance

Contents

CONTENTS

Part 4: Reckoning Illustrated: The Cody Chronicles

Part 5: Lifelong Love and Surrender

Preface

SOON AFTER I YIELDED to the gospel of Jesus Christ, my cousin Bard Pillette gave me a pamphlet on biblical reckoning. I read it but didn't quite grasp the power of the concept until years later. As I look back now, that pamphlet planted a seed. Over time, as that seed was fed by the word of God and watered by the Holy Spirit, it took on the power to transform my life.

Comparison with a mustard seed is apt, because reckoning is cousin of faith. As Jesus said in his famous metaphor, faith even as tiny as a mustard seed can move mountains. Faith and reckoning teamed up in my life to remove a few mountains of sin patterns. I've taught the principle of reckoning in Romans 6:11 over the years, and now through this book I'm able to share this remarkable truth with you.

Here is how this book came to be, in both method and content. For thirty-six years I directed the publications program of the ERIC Clearinghouse on Educational Management at the University of Oregon. For ten years, 1975 to 1985, I also served as pastor of Orchard Community Church in Eugene, and since then I have continued to study and teach the Bible in small groups and mentor young people. This book comes from the mind of a professional research analyst and the heart of a pastor.

At the university I developed a method of information analysis to make the results of educational research available to K-12 school leaders. My staff and I gleaned the best ideas from research on school leadership and summarized them for principals and superintendents across the nation. We tried to combine research findings and the best aspects of theory with practical recommendations for action. In this book I use that same method to explain the principle of reckoning and demonstrate how you can apply it to your life.

The book's focal point is Paul's command in Romans 6:11, but I have also taken a wide-angle view of all Scripture, because reckoning shows up some places we might least expect it. Chapter 2 offers one example, where the theme of this book can be seen in the dress of the young volunteers David foresaw in Psalm 110. We must also avoid reckoning wrong conceptions of ourselves, as chapter 5 warns in regard to Darwinian evolution. In chapter 1, setting one Bible passage in juxtaposition with another amplifies a key topic, in this case the gospel. Chapter 8 examines reckoning in Abraham's life. And in chapter 16, six little words in Hebrews 2:10 reveal the heart of God and inspire a lifetime of reckoning ourselves alive to him.

I have tried to portray reckoning through illustration and example, and that is why the interaction between Cody and Lonny in part 4 occupies the center of the book. People have asked me if Cody is an actual person. No, he's not, but he is in some ways a composite of people I've known, people who are trying to do the best with circumstances beyond their control, initially stumbling, and then yielding to a greater love that captures their heart. The book's clear and concise style makes it suitable for a wide audience.

I am especially grateful to my new friends at Wipf and Stock Publishers for making this book available to you. My hope and prayer are that it now plant a seed in your mind and heart so the power of reckoning can transform your life.

Stuart C. Smith

January 2016

Introduction

M UCH OF MY GROWTH as a Christian came from discovering what God thinks of me. From the time of my conversion I had a hunger to know about God, but I thought he was disappointed in me. How could God like me? I couldn't get free from some sins, and my insecurity kept me from meaningful Christian service. Over time, I began to see how a biblical concept introduced to me at the beginning of my Christian life was the path to freedom.

I needed to see myself not as I thought, or rather *feared*, God sees me, but as God truly does see me. The command of the Apostle Paul in Romans 6:11 to reckon myself dead to sin and alive to God in Christ was the lens that corrected my vision.

Reckoning is counting on something to be true. To reckon in the biblical sense is to think as God does and agree with what he says. We can count on God's word being true, and the Bible says plenty about the status of a believer in Christ. When I began to reckon those things being true about me, something powerful happened.

What does God say about my identity as a believer in Christ? Can I think of myself as righteous? Having trusted in Christ for salvation, am I still to think of myself as a sinner? How does God view me in relationship to him? How am I to think of Satan's influence over me? Answers come as we look to the Bible and think or reckon on its truths.

Our culture avoids the issue of sin and people generally don't like to talk about it or read about it. Taking in your hands this book

1

intended to help people conquer their sin shows that you are willing to go against the cultural grain. More power to you! Chances are that the Holy Spirit is active in your life, because it is he who convicts of sin and guides to holiness. Be encouraged that your interest in this subject is itself a good thing.

If you seek from this book help to conquer your sin, you are on a good quest. If your goal in conquering your sin is to live a life more pleasing to God, that is an excellent desire. And if you want to learn what God is passionate about so you can make his passion your passion, you have arrived at the best motivation of all. As Paul the apostle says, we reckon not only that we are dead to sin, but also *alive to God* (Rom 6:11)—*alive* to his purpose for us.

My purpose in writing this book is to help you do all these things by thinking biblically about God, yourself, and other believers. This book is not a testimonial or personal account of my own experience, about which I say only a little. It does illustrate reckoning in the life of a young believer, but the book's focal point throughout is God's trustworthy Scripture.

You will discover that reckoning plays a key role in sanctification. *Sanctification*, if you are new to the concept, is the process by which believers become more like Christ in thought, word, and deed.

I titled the Summary "A Model for Reckoning." Because this model does not fit neatly within one of the traditional models of sanctification—Reformed, Wesleyan, or Holiness—perhaps it will help you to know some of the assumptions I hold about sanctification. This book adheres to a New Covenant or New Creation model of spirituality (2 Cor 5:17; Col 3:8–10; Eph 4:22–24). Here is what I believe:

- Sanctification is for the believer a lifelong process of transformation into Christlike character, most purely expressed in voluntary, self-giving love.

- Victory over sin is never complete and the believer this side of heaven is never free of temptation, but Christians can live in relative freedom from sin.

- Sanctification is a cooperative activity of both God and believer, the outworking of divine grace and human effort.

- The Holy Spirit sanctifies the believer primarily by making God more attractive and sin less so. The third member of the Trinity both warns against sin and directs eyes to the beauty of Jesus Christ.

- The Bible is alive with the power to cleanse from sin and promote growth.

- Sanctification involves not a contest between two natures (old man versus new man), but rather a life lived in alignment with the Christian's true identity—a born-again child of God with a new heart from which springs the desire to obey God.

- Passivity is a form of self-sabotage. The believer must commit to a ruthless assault on sin and enforce the word of God in one's life.

- Positive conquers negative in the biblical conception of the sanctified life. Walking by the Spirit overcomes deeds of the flesh, virtues replace vices, love for Jesus deflates love for the world, and service to others negates self-centered introspection.

These principles are the themes of this book, and now that you hold it in your hands I invite you to read on and discover the power of biblical reckoning. Learn what God thinks of you as a result of what he has done for you.

Once you see yourself as God sees you, I am convinced by God's authoritative word that you will turn increasingly away from sin and fall more passionately in love with the Father and Jesus the Son.

"The most powerful of all spiritual forces is man's view of himself, the way in which he understands his nature and his destiny, indeed it is the one force which determines all the others which influence human life."[1]

—EMIL BRUNNER, SWISS THEOLOGIAN

1. Brunner, *Christian Understanding of Man*, 146.

PART 1

Volunteering for Christ

BIBLICAL RECKONING IS A command the Apostle Paul gave to those who have already trusted in Jesus Christ for salvation. Before we can reckon, we must first believe. So before exploring the subject of reckoning, I want to give you an opportunity to settle the matter of your salvation.

Sin is a problem for every human being because it is a barrier that prevents relationship with God, now and in eternity. Sin separates us from the holy and pure God, and the penalty of sin is death (Isa 59:2; Ezek 18:4; Rom 6:23).

God took the initiative to rescue humanity by himself becoming a man, Jesus, whose death on the cross paid the penalty for our sin. The message of the gospel—this word literally means *good news*—is that God in his kindness freely offers salvation to every human being who receives Jesus Christ as Savior and Lord (John 3:16).

These two short chapters introduce the gospel and the life that awaits those who volunteer to follow Christ.

In chapter 1, I wonder how one of the Old Testament saints, the author of Psalm 119, might have felt upon hearing that salvation had to come by the death of God's only Son. His first response may well have been disgust, followed by amazement, and then delight. How do you respond? I hope you choose to receive Jesus Christ as your Lord and Savior, and you may do so by means of the included prayer.

If you decide to commit your life to Christ, chapter 2 briefly describes the adventure that awaits you. As one of the Lord's volunteers, you will join his spiritual fight against the enemies of God and of the human soul. This chapter also introduces the book's theme.

1

Two Men and Two Questions
The Gospel of Jesus Christ

NOW, TO HELP ME present the good news of salvation through Jesus Christ, I introduce you to a couple of men. The first man—we don't know his name—lived some three thousand years ago. He had struggled early in his life and then found comfort in God. Later in life, he sought to counsel a younger generation in the riches of God's word, and Psalm 119 is his prayerful testimony. He began the second stanza with this question: "How can a young man keep his way pure?"

Only someone with a strong devotion to God who overcame the many obstacles to a pure life in an impure world would think to pose such a question and then presume to instruct others with his answer. Of course, this man's desire to live righteously was exceptional for the time in which he lived, as it is for anyone in any era who loves God.

About one thousand years later another man wrote a question, this one posed strangely different from the psalmist's: "How can we who died to sin still live in it?" Imagine the response of the psalmist had he been able to gaze into the future and read this question posed by the Apostle Paul to the believers in Rome (Rom 6:2).

The author of Psalm 119 knew very well what sin is, because he was on the receiving end of others' scorn and he was painfully aware of the selfishness and deceit in his own heart.

But the psalmist would have been mystified by the claim that some people in the future would be dead to sin. He had learned to keep sin at bay by his disciplined devotion to Scripture. But how could it be possible that people will actually die to sin?

A Mystery Revealed

It's doubtful the author of Psalm 119 knew that God would become a man named Jesus, live a sinless life, and volunteer to die on a cross. For sure he was familiar with the concept of atonement from having observed the annual ritual of the sins of the people being placed on the scapegoat (Lev 16:8–10).

But God in human flesh taking those sins on himself? And how can God consider those who trust in Jesus to have died *with* Jesus? Paul, are you telling me that those believers can now consider themselves dead to sin and alive to God in Jesus Christ? Alive? Jesus rose from the dead? And his followers rose with him?

Our psalmist friend would have been astonished at all these revelations. He would have considered them impossible, scandalous, even disgusting—that any man, let alone a man who is also God, would have to die for the sins of the people. That was what the blood of goats and calves was for, he would have thought. We know why he would have been confounded and amazed, because the New Testament says the gospel was a mystery.

In the New Testament we learn that our salvation required shedding the blood not of an animal, but the blood of Christ (Heb 9:12). A *mystery*, as the Bible considers it, is something that had been hidden and was revealed. In this sense, both the gospel and Christ himself are mysteries that were hidden from previous generations and were revealed after Jesus died for humanity's sin and rose victoriously from the grave (Eph 6:19; Col 1:26, 2:2; 1 Tim 3:16).

Old Testament saints did not know about the gospel, but they were saved by God's grace through faith just as we believers obtain salvation today, because God applied Jesus' blood retrospectively for the atonement of their sins as for ours (Rom 5:12–19). Being the godly man he was, and being reminded of the many OT passages that point forward to the coming of a Savior who would suffer (Isa 53, for example), I think the author of Psalm 119 would have caught on quickly to the mystery that was unveiled in the gospel of Jesus Christ.

And he would have been delighted to discover in that gospel the ultimate answer to his question, for only by faith in Jesus Christ do young men and women keep their way pure.

Make Your Salvation Sure—Right Now

Here now is how you can put your faith in Jesus Christ.

This is the promise of Scripture: "Everyone who calls on the name of the Lord will be saved" (Rom 10:13). This is a promise to save you from the guilt, condemnation, and spiritual death that come upon every soul who rejects Jesus Christ (Rom 6:23). It is also a promise to give you the many benefits of a heart-to-heart personal relationship with God.

When you call upon the name of the Lord, understand that you will be giving him the deed to your life, because he bought you with the price of his life (1 Cor 6:20), and you will live no longer for yourself but for him who died and was raised for you (2 Cor 5:15). You can talk to God through prayer, saying something like this:

> Dear God, I agree that I have sinned and that I need your forgiveness. I want the salvation you promise. Thank you for sending Jesus to die in my place and make it possible for me to live. Today I call upon you for the gift of salvation through Jesus. I want that gift, and I am making a decision to turn away from my former life of sin. I now pledge my allegiance to you as my Lord. Thank you that you have heard my prayer and saved my soul!

If you prayed this prayer in faith, God is now your heavenly Father and he has adopted you into his family. Jesus Christ considers you his friend and brother. The Holy Spirit, the third member of the Trinity, now indwells you, and he will begin his work of conforming you to the likeness of Jesus.

The Bible teaches us how to grow in our relationship with God. Start reading it regularly, every day if possible, to learn more about your divine Savior.

God's people are an intentional community whose mission is to serve one another and the world, so you will not be spiritually healthy if you remain in isolation from others who have trusted in Christ. Find a Bible-believing and Spirit-filled church where you can be baptized and grow together with other people who cherish Jesus Christ (Phil 3:7–8).

In the next chapter, you will see that you have become one of the young volunteers who fight alongside Lord Jesus as he extends his rule in people's hearts and minds.

2

The Young Volunteers

"The Lord says to my Lord:
'Sit at My right hand
Until I make Your enemies a footstool for Your feet.'
The Lord will stretch forth Your strong scepter
from Zion, saying,
'Rule in the midst of Your enemies.'
Your people will volunteer freely in the day of Your power;
In holy array, from the womb of the dawn,
Your youth are to You as the dew."

(Ps 110:1-3 NASB)

L ONG AGO DAVID, THE great warrior, poet, and king of Israel, was given a prophetic glimpse of the time in which we now live. He saw an army of young volunteers beautifully clothed and united in affection for a future divine ruler. Every day, David's imagery suggests, new volunteers as numerous as drops of morning dew join this army and freely offer their lives in the service of their Lord. David recognized this ruler also as his Lord.

David understood that God the Father ("the Lord") made the following proclamation to David's Lord: "Sit at my right hand, until I make your enemies your footstool." What David wrote about in Psalm 110 was the future rule of Jesus Christ. We know this because Jesus identified himself as the Lord of whom David spoke (Matt 22:41–46).

There are many other references to this psalm in the New Testament. One of them is recorded in the book of Acts. Ten days after Jesus ascended to heaven, the Apostle Peter quoted this psalm in his sermon to thousands of people on the day of Pentecost. He said David foresaw the resurrection of Jesus who is now "exalted at the right hand of God" (Acts 2:31–33).

The youthful volunteers David foresaw are the people God the Father promised would come alongside Jesus Christ as he extends his rule over the earth. If you have believed in him, you are one of those volunteers and this book is for you. There is still time to become one of these royal troops if you have not done so already, as the previous chapter explains.

Assurance of Victory

The army of Christ is his church. You are volunteering not for some religious holy war to be fought with bombs and bullets, but rather for a spiritual struggle against the enemies of God and of the human soul. These enemy forces are lies and unbelief, sin and rebellion, condemnation and death, and an opposing army of evil spirits led by the devil.

Jesus defeated all these foes through his death and resurrection, but their opposition to God and their assault on the human race continue. God, in his wisdom, postponed their destruction until a later age when, as the imagery of the footstool suggests, Christ's enemies will be bound beneath his feet. But for now, God has declared that Christ shall rule not over his enemies but *in the midst* of them (Ps 110:2).

Jesus knows you will encounter these enemy forces and he has equipped you with his word and Spirit to live and fight victoriously. Especially at first, your struggle will be against pockets of resistance inside of you—the sin in your own heart.

One thing you must understand: there is no neutral ground. By aligning with Christ in this war, your victory is assured just as his is assured. Those who do not volunteer are choosing rather to align with the Lord's enemies, and they will suffer a common fate.

The Theme of This Book

Notice the language David used to describe the garments of these volunteers. They are dressed in "holy array" (literally, "holy splendors"). Just as soldiers' uniforms identify the army to which they belong, these holy garments signal the identity of the volunteers. When they join the Lord's army they are given something only the Lord possesses and therefore only he can give: holiness. To understand this is to understand the theme of this book.

The volunteers' dress conveys a profound truth about the spiritual status of people who pledge their allegiance to the Lord. They no longer wear filthy garments of sin, guilt, and shame, because they have now put on the holy and righteous garments of Christ. As Paul phrased it, "You who were baptized into Christ have clothed yourselves with Christ" (Gal 3:27 NASB; Col 3:9–10). If you are one of his volunteers, you stripped off the old rags of guilt and wrapped yourself in Christ's holy splendor. You now display your true identity in Christ.

Here is where all believers, even those of us who have served Christ many years, face a strange reality. We are righteous and holy by means of our identity with Christ, but our battle with sin has not ended. We live in an in-between state. Freed from guilt and declared righteous, we can still be tempted to live as we formerly did. In terms of Paul's clothing metaphor, if we don't feel comfortable in our new holy attire, we may want to retrieve the rags from the trash and return to our former lifestyle. Paul knew this could happen, so in other passages he turned his clothing metaphor into an exhortation.

What the Galatians passage says we have already done we now must continue to do: "clothe yourselves with the Lord Jesus Christ, and do not think about how to gratify the desires of the flesh" (Rom 13:14 NIV); and "put on the new self, created after the likeness of God in true righteousness and holiness" (Eph 4:24).

In reality, God is the one who wrapped us in Christ, and now we are responsible to live in accord with our new identity. Our new self does want to please our Lord. We long for the day when our thoughts and actions will be as pure and clean as our holy garb.

As you read this, you may be caught up now in sin and compromise, but want to change. There is a way of escape. It is a process the Bible calls *sanctification*—a lifelong process of spiritual maturation. You can indeed live in relative freedom from sin, and the first step is to *see and think of yourself as God does*. This is the meaning of *reckoning*.

Reckoning stands at the nexus between accomplished fact and commanded action. God accomplished the fact of your death to sin. He crucified your old self on the cross with Christ (Rom 6:6). Your part is to reckon and obey. You reckon on the fact that you are dead to sin and alive to God. Reckoning gives you the confidence to leave behind the sins of the old self and walk into the freedom of your new self. Reckoning is your first decisive step on the pathway to freedom.

PART 2

Reckoning Defined

RECKONING IS A TYPE of thinking that recognizes or takes into account what is true. Everyone considers some things true—even if they are not true—so everyone reckons. Biblical reckoning recognizes the truth of what God has done to free his people from sin and make them alive to worship him.

Reckoning is not a clever way of thinking, nor is it an option for followers of Christ. Romans 6:11 is a *command* by the Apostle Paul to reckon ourselves dead to sin and alive to God in Jesus Christ.

Chapter 3 defines biblical reckoning as thinking of ourselves as God does. We can reckon ourselves dead to sin and alive to God because God considers us united with Christ in his death and resurrection. God credits righteousness to the account of everyone who trusts in Jesus Christ for salvation.

Chapter 4 explains how to align our thinking with what it means to be a saint, to be born again with a new heart, to be a child of God, and to participate in Christ's victory over Satan.

We must distinguish reckoning what God declares to be true from reckoning false conceptions of ourselves that we pick up from other people, the culture, or Satan's accusations. One such false conception, explored in chapter 5, is that human beings appeared on this planet as the result of Darwinian evolution.

Dear Father, I ask that you help me to see myself as you see me. I want to think of myself as you do, forgiven and without shame, accepted by your pure heart of love, in your beloved Son. Please give me by the Holy Spirit the spirit of wisdom and revelation of who you are so I can know you. Expand my vision, Father. Amen.

3

Thinking God's Thoughts

*"Likewise you also, reckon yourselves to be
dead indeed to sin,*

but alive to God in Christ Jesus our Lord"

(ROM 6:11 NKJ)

M Y PURPOSE IN WRITING this book is to help you understand
how God thinks of you and sees you so that you can think of
yourself as he does. What God thinks of you depends on whether
you have trusted in Jesus Christ. If you have not yet taken this
all-important first step, I encourage you to go back a few pages to
chapter 1 and call on the name of the Lord.

We begin our exploration of reckoning with the example of a
young man who some five hundred years ago discovered the gift of
salvation and learned to think of himself as righteous.

The Gift of Righteousness

In the summer of 1505, Martin Luther was in his early twenties and
had just enrolled in law school, having already earned his master's
degree. A young man of tender conscience, Luther was insecure
about his salvation and feared God's judgment. Maybe his fear was
heightened by having seen two of his brothers die of the plague.

One day in July of that year, Luther was on horseback when a lightning bolt struck near him during a thunderstorm. Terrified of God's judgment, he dropped out of law school and joined a monastery, hoping to find peace for his soul. He devoted himself to life as a monk, fasting, praying, making confession, studying the Bible, and even flagellating himself. But doubts and fear still plagued Luther.

Ten years later, when Luther was studying Paul's letter to the believers in Rome, he found the answer to his despair in this statement: "The righteous shall live by faith."

Luther had read these words in the first chapter of Romans before but did not understand them. Assuming Paul meant that God *demanded* people to be righteous, Luther had lived in fear that he could not meet God's standard of righteousness. Now he realized what Paul actually meant: God freely *gives* his righteousness to those who receive the gospel by faith. As Luther put it, Paul speaks of the "righteousness that God makes available to us who are not righteous."[1]

This lightning bolt of truth consumed Luther's fear and doubt. He wrote, "When I understood that, and when the concept of justification by faith alone burst through into my mind, suddenly it was like the doors of paradise swung open and I walked through."[2]

Luther finally discovered the core message of the Christian gospel: unrighteous people are declared righteous—justified—by faith in Jesus Christ. Justification is by grace alone through faith alone. Because this gift is given to those who are not righteous, Luther called it "an alien righteousness, a foreign righteousness, that is granted to us for our own possession."[3]

I hope you have already made the same discovery of righteousness by faith that Luther did. If so, you know that you do not need to labor and sacrifice for this righteousness, because God offers it as a gift. Having accepted that gift by faith, you are now seeking to put your faith into practice as a follower of Christ.

1. Cited by Sproul, *Gospel of God*, 14.
2. Ibid.
3. Ibid.

Our Paradise in Christ

We can see why Luther called the believer's righteousness "a foreign righteousness," because it does not originate inside us but is a gift that arrives by something God did for us and declares true of us. It is not a pretend righteousness, but truly is the righteousness of Christ.

We, like Luther, may liken our discovery of the gift of righteousness to walking through the doors of paradise. Those doors open even wider when we understand the amazing gift of being *in Christ*.

In chapter 6 of Romans, the truth of justification by faith that Luther discovered takes on practical meaning. The Apostle Paul explains that we died with Christ, and therefore we are no longer under the domination of sin. We also rose from the grave with Christ, so we are now free to live righteously with him.

The truths in Romans 6 and many other Bible passages say something important about our identity, and how our identity shapes the way we are to live as followers of Christ. We need to know how God defines our identity so we can define ourselves as he does.

"In Christ" in God's Thoughts

Wayne Grudem states this about believers: "Throughout Christ's entire life on earth, from the time of his birth to the time of his ascension into heaven, God thought of us as being 'in Christ.' That is, whatever Christ did as our representative, God counted it as being something we did, too."[4]

We did nothing apart from our faith to attain this status, because it is something God assigns us, as Grudem makes clear: "believers were present in Christ *only in God's thoughts*. God *thought of us* as going through everything that Christ went through, because he was our representative"[5] (his emphasis).

4. Grudem, *Systematic Theology*, 841.
5. Ibid.

Jesus' obedience became our obedience, in God's eyes. When Jesus died on the cross, we died with him. "In the same way, God thought of us as having been *buried* with Christ, *raised* with him, and *taken up to heaven* with him in glory" (his emphasis).[6] Grudem continues:

> When Christ returned to heaven, therefore, all the blessings of salvation were earned for us. God thought of these blessings as being rightfully ours, just as if we had earned them ourselves. Nevertheless, they were stored up for us in heaven—in God's mind, actually, and in Christ, our representative—waiting to be applied to us personally (1 Peter 1:3–5; Col. 3:3–4; Eph. 1:3).[7]

Now that we understand how God thinks of us, the next step is to apply these truths to our lives. We do this through reckoning. Note that Grudem says God "counted" what Christ did as something we did also. As I will explain in a moment, *counted* has the same meaning as *reckoned*. God reckoned us doing all these things in Christ as our representative, and now he invites us—indeed, commands us—to reckon the same thing. Through Paul God gave the command to reckon ourselves dead to sin and alive to God in Christ Jesus (Rom 6:11).

Reckoning Ourselves Righteous

The Greek word that is translated *reckon,* or in some translations *count* or *consider,* is *logizomai.* You will notice that the first several letters correspond with the English word *logic,* which has to do with thinking. Lexicons typically define the Greek verb with such English words as "to count, reckon, calculate, think, consider." One authoritative lexicon includes the phrase *"look upon as"* and states that the form of the verb in Romans 6:11 yields the meaning *"look*

6. Ibid., 842.
7. Ibid.

upon someone as.[8] We are to *look upon ourselves as* dead to sin and alive to God in Christ.

Reckoning is a concept that comes from the world of mathematics and accounting, and here is what the Bible wants us to know: when we believe in Christ for salvation, God deposits in our spiritual bank account the righteousness of Christ and all the blessings that come from being in him. We draw from the riches in our account by reckoning these blessings ours. It's like writing a check when we know that we have money in our account.

Paul uses the word *reckoning* to make the point that righteousness comes by faith. In Galatians 3:6, for example, Paul quotes Genesis 15:6: "Abraham believed God, and it was reckoned to him for righteousness" (NASB). Note that it was God who reckoned Abraham righteous on the basis of his faith. Because God reckoned Abraham righteous, Abraham was entitled to reckon himself righteous, as we will see in more detail in chapter 8.

R. C. Sproul says that when Paul commands us to reckon ourselves dead to sin and alive to God, he is telling us "to think of yourselves in this way." Sproul explains:

> Paul is making here a very simple deduction. If God reckons you dead in Jesus Christ, if God accounts your sins to be dead on the cross, then you also ought to reckon yourself to be dead. Paul is not asking us to do anything toward ourselves that God has not first done for us. We are to consider that our old life is dead. Put it away, it's over, it's done. It died once and for all. You can't go back.[9]

Because the command is given with apostolic authority, it should not be treated as frivolous, says Everett Harrison in his commentary on Romans. Nor should it "be undertaken in a mechanical fashion," he writes, "as though there were some sort of magic in going through the motions. One must really desire to have freedom from sin and to live responsibly to God."[10]

8. Arndt and Gingrich, *Greek-English Lexicon*, 477.

9. Sproul, *Gospel of God*, 113–14.

10. Harrison, *Romans*, 71.

You may be wondering about now where the power of reckoning comes from. How can reckoning help us conquer sin and live fully alive to God? Before I answer that question, I must distinguish biblical reckoning from another kind of thinking that has gained popularity.

Do We Create Our Own Reality?

A maxim of the modern self-help movement is that people can create their own reality by controlling how they think. Here, for example, is a familiar claim found on a personal development website: "The power to change your world rests within yourself—within your mind!" Some pastors and consultants today still preach the power of positive thinking made famous by Norman Vincent Peale: "Change your thoughts and you change your world."

So is reckoning a form of positive thinking or one of many mind-control techniques for thinking our way to a better world? Not at all. Rather than create a new reality for ourselves by reimagining our circumstances, biblical reckoning acknowledges what God has done to change our lives. God made us dead to sin and alive to God through our union with Christ in his death and resurrection. Try creating that reality!

As Harrison states, "Reckoning does not create the fact of union with Christ but makes it operative in one's life."[11] This same point is expressed well by N. T. Wright:

> The "reckoning" in question is to take place in the believing thought processes of the Christian. . . . The point is not, as in some schemes of piety, that the "reckoning" *achieves* the result of dying to sin and coming alive to God, any more than someone adding up a column of figures creates the result out of nothing; it opens the eyes of mind and heart to recognize what is in fact true.[12]

11. Ibid.
12. Cited by Kruse, *Romans*, 267.

Changing the way we think about ourselves may well have the power to make friends and influence people, and it could even land us a job. But human imagination, thought, and volition can only take us so far in life. To the extent we might be able to change our world by changing our thoughts, our "world" would have to be quite small.

Reckoning's Transforming Power

The power of reckoning, in contrast to mind-control techniques, comes from believing and acting on what God has done for us. This kind of thinking is based on fact, not imagination. We do not invent reality; we reckon on the reality that God brought into existence by uniting us with Christ in his death and resurrection. This kind of thinking truly has the power to renew our lives (Rom 6:4).[13]

Reckoning's power lies in its ability to enforce what faith began. Reckoning follows faith. On the basis of faith, God declares us dead to sin and alive to him. Now reckoning takes over and insists that what God declares to be true must become real in our experience. We can speak of reckoning as *insistent faith* because it enforces the status that faith brought about.

In the face of temptation to sin, reckoning says I am dead to that. In terms of intimacy with God and pleasing him, reckoning says I am alive to that. Reckoning positions our mind and will to carry out Paul's command in the very next verse, which is to not let sin reign in our mortal body to make us obey its passions (6:12).

---

13. The efficacy of reckoning to renew the mind is supported by research on the plasticity of the human brain. As Caroline Leaf discusses in *Switch on Your Brain* (Baker, 2013), thoughts can alter the structure of the brain through a process called *epigenetics*. Leaf writes, "As we think, we change the physical nature of our brain. As we consciously direct our thinking, we can wire out toxic patterns of thinking and replace them with healthy thoughts. New thought networks grow" (20). She points to the brain's neuroplasticity as scientific evidence for the renewal Paul writes about in Romans 12:2. "It is with our minds that we change the physical reality of the brain to reflect our choices. It is with our minds that we decide to follow God's rules and live in peace despite what is going on around us" (22).

Reckoning is the launch point for decisive action to make real in our experience what God has declared to be true. It enforces in our thought life what God has said about us, and thought becomes father of action. The Holy Spirit beckons us to use this power of enforcement to remove everything that stands in the way of satisfying our heart's desire for intimacy with God. Do you know, my friend, that you have a new heart that adores God and hungers for his presence? Reckoning opens a window to discover this new heart and give it free expression in your life.

Our union with Christ is the source of every spiritual blessing we enjoy. In the next chapter, we will look at more of the amazing rewards that come from being in Christ, for in him we discover our true identity.

"You are not what you think you are. There is a glory to your life that your Enemy fears, and he is hell-bent on destroying that glory before you act on it.

This part of the answer will sound unbelievable at first; perhaps it will sound too good to be true; certainly, you will wonder if it is true for you.

But once you begin to see with those eyes, once you have begun to know it is true from the bottom of your heart, it will change everything."

—JOHN ELDREDGE[14]

14. Eldredge, *Waking the Dead*, 33–34.

4

A New Identity in Christ

THE MOMENT WE TRUSTED in Christ our identity underwent radical change. God instantly united us with Christ and declared us righteous. Important as these blessings are, the Bible tells of even more favors God bestows on those who believe in his Son.

We were transformed from dead to alive, from darkness to light, from condemned sinner to justified saint, from enemy of God to his friend, from child of wrath to righteous and beloved child of God, from outcast and alien to member of the church, the body of Christ.

Nevertheless, these gifts may not immediately change the way we think or the way we live. You may read these things and think to yourself, "None of this makes sense because it isn't anything like what I experience. I am anything but righteous, my desires are far from godly, and in no way could I be called a saint." Please hear this, my friend: the challenge you face is to believe what the Bible says about you.

To help you match your thinking with your new identity, this chapter explores what it means to be a saint, to be born again with a new heart, to be a child of God, and to participate in Christ's victory over Satan.

Sinners or Saints?

Often Christians refer to themselves as "sinners saved by grace," but is that the way the Bible characterizes believers? Should we consider ourselves sinners who only sometimes live as saints, or saints who sometimes sin? These questions take us to the heart of biblical reckoning.

We have seen that God declares us to be righteous, so we must reckon this to be true. The Bible also calls us *saints*, meaning *holy ones* or people *set apart*. The word *saint* has the same Greek root as *sanctification*, which has three meanings in the Bible.

First, *saint* has the meaning of being set apart from the world and dedicated for service to God; this is *relational sanctification*. For example, Jesus in his prayer to the Father in John 17 spoke of his own consecration for service to do the Father's will when he said, "I sanctify myself." Then he prayed for his disciples to be set apart for their service; his prayer was "that they also may be sanctified by the truth" (John 17:19 NKJ).

Second is *progressive sanctification*—the process of spiritual maturation that follows being born again and continues until we are glorified in Christ. As we'll see in chapter 6, we cooperate with the Holy Spirit in this ongoing process.

Third, all believers enjoy the standing in God's sight of having been cleansed from sin by Christ's death. This may be what Paul meant when he reminded the believers in Corinth of their past sinful states and then said, "Such were some of you; but you were washed, but you were sanctified, but you were justified in the name of the Lord Jesus Christ and in the Spirit of our God" (1 Cor 6:11 NASB; also see Heb 10:10). Here sanctification is an accomplished fact, so we can also speak of a *positional sanctification* that derives from our union with Christ.

Everyone who is in Christ can be called a saint in this three-fold sense: (1) every believer is set apart for service to God; (2) every believer over his or her lifetime is progressing toward maturity; and (3) God in his sovereign plan sees every believer as already having been sanctified (purified and holy). For all these reasons, the New Testament commonly refers to all believers as saints, such as when Paul tells the Roman believers to receive Phoebe "in the Lord in a manner worthy of the saints" (Rom 16:2).

Saint describes not our behavior but our standing—as God thinks of us and sees us and as he wants us to see ourselves. This is how God thinks of you now, even if only a few minutes ago you followed my advice in chapter 1 and called on the Lord to be saved. Because you died with Christ and rose from the grave with him, you are no longer to think of yourself as a sinner saved by grace but as a saint becoming more free from sin and more like Christ.

Of course, I am not saying that you will no longer sin or that you have no responsibility to resist sin. The Bible makes it very clear that our behavior must change to align with our position as saints: "Since we have these promises, beloved, let us cleanse ourselves from every defilement of body and spirit, bringing holiness to completion in the fear of God" (2 Cor 7:1). We are even told to be holy as God is holy (1 Pet 1:16).

Our positional sanctification is great incentive to put effort into our progressive sanctification. Knowing all that the Father and Son have done for us, we want to please them and bring honor to their name. We want to discover their desire and make it our desire, embrace their passion as our passion. This godly mindset well expresses what it means to reckon ourselves alive to God, as Cody discovers in chapters 13–15.

Let us explore a bit further our identity as believers, looking next at being born again, which is the meaning of *regenerated*.

Born Again

We find another aspect of our identity in the important biblical term *regeneration*. Regeneration means *rebirth* or *new birth* and is the bestowal of a new heart with the ability to obey God. It takes place the moment we trust in Christ. To be regenerated is to be born again, bringing a dramatic change in both our identity and the impulses of our heart. Paul said we who are in Christ are "a

new creation. The old has passed away; behold, the new has come"
(2 Cor 5:17 NASB).

A new heart is a feature of the New Covenant that was proph-
esied by Jeremiah (31:33–34) and by Ezekiel, who called it a new
heart and a new spirit (36:26). With this new heart comes a change
in the desires of our heart. We used to ignore or even hate Jesus
Christ, but now we love him and want to be near him. "Though
you have not seen him, you love him" (1 Pet 1:8). John Piper addresses this theme:

> Saving faith is the cry of a new creature in Christ. And
> the newness of the new creature is that it has a new taste.
> What was once distasteful or bland is now craved. Christ
> Himself has become a Treasure Chest of holy joy. The tree
> of faith grows only in the heart that craves the supreme
> gift that Christ died to give: not health, not wealth, not
> prestige—but God![1]

The new birth also changes our desire toward sin: "No one
born of God makes a practice of sinning, for God's seed abides in
him, and he cannot keep on sinning because he has been born of
God" (1 John 3:9). John is not saying that we who are born again
never sin. Rather, our new heart instinctively turns away from sin.
Unregenerated people, in contrast, have a different spiritual father
who imparts a different set of desires. Jesus told those who were
opposed to his teaching, "You are of your father the devil, and your
will is to do your father's desires" (John 8:44).

We who are born of God can still do evil things, but the incli-
nation of our heart makes us no longer content to keep on sinning.
In contrast, people who have not been born again can do many
good things while remaining comfortable in their sin. Again refer-
ring to people who opposed him, Jesus said, "For out of the heart
come evil thoughts, murder, adultery, sexual immorality, theft,
false witness, slander" (Matt 15:19).

The new birth implanted a new desire for godliness, and as we
nurture that new desire we find ourselves less attracted to former

---

1. Piper, *Desiring God*, 72–73.

ways of thinking and behaving. We become so attuned to God that we want to please him even with our innermost thoughts, as David prayed: "Let the words of my mouth and the meditation of my heart be acceptable in Your sight, O Lord, my strength and my Redeemer" (Ps 19:14 NKJ).

David realized that God could see into his inner world and could renew even his thoughts and intentions in such a way as to make them pleasing to God.

These godly desires increase over time as we grow in sanctification, but for the rest of our life we will still have to deal with the temptations and enticements to sin, in both thought and deed. When we sin (not *if* we sin), we need to confess our sin to God for forgiveness and cleansing from unrighteousness so we can be restored to fellowship (1 John 1:9).

Paul tells us to "put on the new self, created after the likeness of God in true righteousness and holiness" (Eph 4:24; see also Col 3:12–17). God has given us this new self, but we still have a responsibility: we must reckon it ours and put it on.

Accepted into God's Family

Every believer is a child of God. We derive our identity and name from our heavenly Father, Paul says in Ephesians 3:14–15. See how exuberantly John expresses this identity: "See what great love the Father has lavished on us, that we should be called children of God! And that is what we are!" (1 John 3:1 NIV).

Paul refers to our privileged status as the Father's adopted sons: "For you did not receive the spirit of slavery to fall back into fear, but you have received the Spirit of adoption as sons, by whom we cry, 'Abba! Father!'" (Rom 8:15).

In the Roman world, a childless rich man would adopt a young adult male of good character to inherit the rich man's wealth and maintain his family name. The adopted son could expect to enjoy a privileged life free of hardship. As J. I. Packer notes in his *Concise Theology*, God, in contrast, adopts sons lacking character to impart in them the character of Jesus. As a requirement for our inheritance, we must endure hardship as discipline (Heb 12:7–10; Rom 8:17).

Why is gender important? Why doesn't Paul, like John, use the neutral term *child* instead of *son*? The reason is that Paul writes about the children as heirs, with the understanding that the inheritance goes to the son. Nevertheless, all believers, male and female, will share equally in God's estate. Men are also the bride of Christ!

Authority over the Devil

Christ's victory over evil spiritual forces has become our victory. Because we are in Christ, we are set free from the domination of Satan.

Following his ascension, Jesus Christ sat down at the right hand of the Father in heaven, far above all other powers and authorities (Eph 1:20–21). We are there seated "with him in the heavenly places in Christ Jesus, so that in the coming ages he might show the immeasurable riches of his grace in kindness toward us in Christ Jesus" (2:6–7).

Jesus Christ came to destroy the works of the devil (1 John 3:8; Heb 2:14), and he triumphed over satanic principalities and powers (Col 2:15). Through the victory of Jesus, we are able to stand "in the Lord" against the schemes of the devil (Eph 6:10–20).

Reckoning is a powerful weapon of spiritual warfare for two reasons.

First, sin is the devil's playground. The devil—Paul refers to him as the "prince of the power of the air"— is an energizing power for sin in the sense that he "works in" or energizes sinners to disobey God and indulge the lusts of the flesh (Eph 2:1–3). "Whoever makes a practice of sinning is of the devil, for the devil has been sinning from the beginning" (1 John 3:8). Reckoning ourselves dead to sin is therefore protection against the devil's temptations.

Second, we reckon Christ's victory over the devil as our victory because of our position in Christ, as the above verses state. To put on the whole armor of God, as Paul commands in Ephesians 6, is itself an act of reckoning. We have already been given truth (the belt), righteousness (the breastplate), the gospel of peace (the boots), faith (the shield), salvation (the helmet), and the word of God (the sword of the Spirit).

These pieces of armor are standard issue for every believer and they come with our position in Christ. By putting them on as an act of faith, we are reckoning these spiritual blessings ours, and this is how we make our stand and maintain our ground against the enemy's assault. We enter the battle in the strength of the Lord and with the authority of his name.

And what are some of the devil's schemes? The devil deceives unbelievers "from seeing the light of the gospel of the glory of Christ, who is the image of God" (2 Cor 4:4). The devil tempts believers to disobey God, and when we do sin the devil tries to slime our minds with guilt and shame and a sense of unworthiness.

In truth, God fully forgave each and every one of us when we trusted in Christ, because God the Father sees us *in Christ*. He loves and accepts us just as he loves and cherishes his dearly beloved Son. Knowing this, we can speak of God's attitude toward us as David did: "he rescued me, because he delighted in me" (Ps 18:19).

Stepping into Freedom

Now that Christ has set us free from sin and Satan, we want to live in alignment with our new identity. As Paul says, "For freedom Christ has set us free; stand firm therefore, and do not submit again to a yoke of slavery" (Gal 5:1). Neither you nor I will attain sinlessness this side of heaven. But sin does not have to rule in our thoughts and actions. We are a new creation with a new heart that is set free to serve and love God as his beloved children. Count—reckon!—all these blessings yours, my friend, and do not let false voices deceive you.

5

God's Image Bearers

W E HAVE SEEN THAT when we trusted in Jesus Christ for salvation, God declared us righteous and placed us "in Christ." He also gave us a new heart with new desires, adopted us into his family, freed us from Satan's grip, and began the process of sanctification. We are a new creation; the old has passed away and the new has come (2 Cor 5:17).

Along with these blessings, God freed us from the control of sin so we can live righteously. Reckoning on the fact of what God has done is now our responsibility. Reckoning is how we put our faith into practice; it is how *given* righteousness becomes *lived* righteousness.

Now we step back briefly to examine another basic belief about our identity: where human beings came from. Our assumptions about human origins are just as much a matter of faith and reckoning as our spiritual identity. We will also see that our belief in either divine creation or Darwinian evolution has implications for how we live.

Created or Mutated?

Where did we come from? Are we the handiwork of God or the result of random mutation and natural selection? Either way, the answer requires an exercise of faith that intertwines with the issue of personal holiness.

Genesis 1:27 records that "God created man in his own image; in the image of God he created him; male and female he created them." Creation in God's image assigns a very different identity to us than if we result from a random process of evolution as now taught in most public schools. This issue requires attention, because it can deter some people from even considering Christianity.

Young people today grow up in a society having a largely secular worldview. To follow Jesus Christ in Western society is to row upstream against a strong current of secular assumptions about the nature of humanity and the world in which we live.

The truth claim of the Bible is that God created all that is, that humanity fell into sin, and that at a particular time in history God became a man and died for humanity's sins so that those who believe in him would live eternally in fellowship with him. But why would people investigate these truth claims of Christianity if they believe the Bible has been disproved by science as defined by the naturalistic and secular worldview that dominates universities.

The False Voice of Darwinism

Darwinian evolution is commonly assumed to be the proved scientific cause for humanity's origin, but there is reason on scientific grounds alone to question this assumption.

More than nine hundred scientists of various disciplines have questioned the legitimacy of Darwinism by putting their signature to the following statement: "We are skeptical of claims for the ability of random mutation and natural selection to account for the complexity of life. Careful examination of the evidence for Darwinian theory should be encouraged." You can read more about these scientists at this website: www.dissentfromdarwin.org/.[1]

---

1. You can also explore the evidence for intelligent design that has accumulated in recent decades at www.intelligentdesign.org/. Among many other widely available critiques of Darwinism, Dr. Geoffrey Simmons, who was for several years my primary care physician, wrote *What Darwin Didn't Know* (Harvest House, 2004) and *Billions of Missing Links* (Harvest House, 2007).

My good friend Douglas Groothuis offers a detailed critique of Darwinian naturalism in his book *Christian Apologetics*. He cites Richard Lewontin, an eminent biologist and defender of Darwinism who makes a candid admission:

> It is not that the methods and institutions of science somehow compel us to accept a material explanation of the phenomenal world, but, on the contrary, that we are forced by our *a priori* adherence to material causes to create an apparatus of investigation and a set of concepts that produce material explanations, no matter how counterintuitive, no matter how mystifying to the uninitiated. Moreover, that materialism is an absolute, for we cannot allow a Divine Foot in the door.[2]

Great scientists of the past have welcomed that Divine Foot. Nicholas Copernicus, Sir Francis Bacon, Johannes Kepler, Galileo Galilei, René Descartes, Blaise Pascal, Isaac Newton, Robert Boyle, and Michael Faraday are among the founders of modern science who believed in God or were committed followers of Jesus Christ. Albert Einstein did not believe in a personal God but is nevertheless famous for saying, "Science without religion is lame, religion without science is blind."[3]

God is the Author of both the material world (Francis Bacon referred to it as "the book of God's Works") and the Bible ("the book of God's Words"). Informed Christians freely examine both books, knowing they will not contradict each other. It is modern materialistic science that keeps one book closed.

The choice between materialism and creation by an intelligent designer is not a choice between reason and faith, as secularists would want you to think, but rather a choice between faith in an unseen process and faith in God. Darwinism, as Groothuis states, "runs more on evidential fumes and a commitment to philosophical materialism than it does on hard empirical evidence or good arguments."[4]

2. Cited by Groothuis, *Christian Apologetics*, 279.
3. Einstein, *Science, Philosophy and Religion*, II.
4. Groothuis, 296.

Here is the assertion of Scripture: "By faith we understand that the universe was created by the word of God, so that what is seen was not made out of things that are visible" (Heb 11:3). Jesus Christ was the agent of creation (Col 1:17), and some 2000 years ago he walked on the planet he created and interacted with people bearing his image.

Destined for Holiness

What does our identity as image bearers of God have to do with personal holiness? This question takes us to the stark difference between the destiny of redeemed humanity as decreed by God and the destination for humanity as envisioned by materialists.

Christians are on a journey toward a sure destination, knowing that we were created to be like God in righteousness and holiness (Eph 4:24). We know that we will see Jesus in his full glory and will be like him, and this hope fuels our desire to live in purity now (1 John 3:2–3).

But if human beings are merely the result of time, matter, chance, and natural law (begging the question where these things came from), then human behavior is subject to a mechanical process with no basis for hope and devoid of moral absolutes. With no accountability to a higher being, societies construct and alter moral codes on the fly, much as we see happening in the United States today.

Death according to the materialist ends in nothingness, not only for each individual after death but also for humanity in general. J.P. Moreland points out that Charles Darwin himself was aware of humanity's hopeless future according to his theory. Realizing the sun will in time grow too cold to sustain life on the planet, Darwin wrote in his autobiography: "Believing as I do that man in the distant future will be a far more perfect creature than he now is, it is an intolerable thought that he and all other sentient beings are doomed to complete annihilation after such a long-continued slow progress."[5]

Death according to the word of God brings judgment and eternal punishment for the unsaved, materialists included, whereas for those who trust in Christ it is the continuation of an eternal adventure. All of saved humanity will dwell in everlasting, joyful fellowship with God the Father, Jesus the God-Man, and one another in the new heaven and new earth (Rev 21:1–3).

At this stage in our journey of faith we are lovers of God who sometimes sin. Now let's get to work, by God's continuing grace in the power of the Holy Spirit, on reducing the frequency of the "sometimes." That process, sanctification, is the subject of part 3.

5. Cited by Moreland, *Kingdom Triangle*, 52.

PART 3

Reckoning Applied

RECKONING IS A COMMAND that must be obeyed. The remarkable thing about this command is that it is not something to do but something to *think*. This thought is so powerful, however, that it inevitably leads to action. Paul's command in Romans 6:11 links thought, faith, and the human will in a partnership to make real in our experience what God has already done through the death and resurrection of Jesus Christ.

Because we are commanded to reckon ourselves dead to sin and alive to God, we must consider how to resist sin and live for God by the power of the Holy Spirit. So chapter 6 describes how reckoning operates in relation to sanctification, the nature of sin, and walking by the Spirit. We learn that we overcome the power of sin by a stronger power and the desire to sin by a stronger desire.

Did Paul speak pessimistically about his own ability to conquer sin? Current scholarship on Romans 7 gives us an answer, as chapter 7 explains.

The life of Abraham is Scripture's clearest example of the power and operation of faith and reckoning. In chapter 8 you will see how reckoning can release the same creative power of faith in your life as it did in Abraham's life.

As an antidote to passivity, chapter 9 offers encouragement to enforce the word of God in your life so that what you reckon to be true becomes real in your experience.

"Therefore there is now no condemnation for those who are in Christ Jesus. For the law of the Spirit of life in Christ Jesus has set you free from the law of sin and of death." (Rom 8:1-2)

"As obedient children, do not be conformed to the passions of your former ignorance, but as he who called you is holy, you also be holy in all your conduct, since it is written, 'You shall be holy, for I am holy'." (1 Pet 1:14-16)

6

Our Responsibility to Resist Sin and Walk by the Spirit

IN SAVING US, GOD did something that we cannot do by ourselves. He freed us from the control of sin and made us alive to God in Christ. Now we can resist sin (which we were unable to do before) and live for God (which we had no desire to do before). In Christ we are freed from sin, no longer its slave.

As we have seen, however, freedom from the control of sin is not the same as victory over sin in our experience. Reckoning ourselves dead to sin is the beginning of a process. Paul's command to reckon in Romans 6:11 is followed by his command not to sin in verse 12. Reckoning comes before doing. The sequence of these commands is, as Harrison points out, "psychologically sound, for what we think tends to be carried out in action. The thought is father to the act."[1]

In this chapter, we move from thought to action, from the knowledge of what God has done for us to what is now our responsibility. We consider what we must do to stand firm against every form of sin.

---

1. Harrison, *Romans*, 71.

God-Dependent Obedience

As we saw in chapter 4, *progressive sanctification* is the process by which Christians increasingly exemplify the character of Christ. Sanctification is a cooperative activity, a partnership between God and us. For our responsibility in this process, we look for the Bible's commands and dedicate ourselves to obeying them in reliance on the Holy Spirit's power. As we learn what God expects of us we put effort into doing what he says.

J. I. Packer well expresses the cooperative nature of our growth into a new life: "God's method of sanctification is neither activism (self-reliant activity) nor apathy (God-reliant passivity), but God-dependent effort (2 Cor. 7:1; Phil. 3:10–14; Heb. 12:14)."[2]

Effort is certainly an appropriate word to describe this man's life: "I have fought the good fight, I have finished the race, I have kept the faith"—the Apostle Paul near the end of his life, writing in 2 Timothy 4:7.

Martyn Luther, as we saw in chapter 3, could not by his discipline win God's acceptance. No one can. Yet the Spirit-filled life is one of mental discipline: "For those who live according to the flesh set their minds on the things of the flesh, but those who live according to the Spirit set their minds on the things of the Spirit" (Rom 8:5). How, then, does discipline fit in with the New Covenant life in the Spirit?

As we saw in part 2, our new heart loves God, desires his presence, and wants to obey him and live by the Spirit. Our new heart hates sin. When we need to know the will of God or face a moral quandary, our new heart, instructed by the word of God, knows the correct choice.

Why, then, do we too often not make the correct choice? Why do we still disobey God and struggle with sin? With a new heart and the Holy Spirit on our side, it seems we should be a lot further along in our sanctification than we are. God could have given us the obedient heart of Jesus the instant we were saved, but he didn't.

---

2. Packer, *Concise Theology,* "Sanctification."

Instead, he wants us to fight for it. Just as Jesus learned obedience through his sufferings (Heb 5:8), so too must we.

The tools he has given us are sufficient for the fight. The indwelling Holy Spirit enables us to obey God and put away sin (Rom 8:4, 13). And our new heart provides the desire to exercise spiritual disciplines, including prayer, worship, study and reading of Scripture, and fellowship with other believers. These disciplines are also our heartfelt response to the mercy and grace of God. We want to please him who saved us; we do not want to grieve him.

In the remainder of this chapter, I will draw attention to what I believe are the most important actions we can take to deal with sin and accelerate our sanctification. We begin with the renewal of our mind by exposing it to God's truth.

The Renewal of Our Mind by the Word

In the New Covenant, God renews both hearts and minds (Jer 31:33). This initial renewal, however, is just the beginning of a life-long process, because the renewed mind is both a gift of God and an ongoing responsibility of every believer.

In Romans 12:2, Paul tells us to be transformed by the re-newing of our minds. The very fact that a human being can have a *renewed* mind is a stunning revelation. To understand why, it's helpful to trace the progression of Paul's thought in Romans. In chapter 1, verse 21, he says people in this fallen world are born with a natural mind that refuses to honor God or give him thanks. Their thinking is futile, and their hearts are foolish and darkened. All of those charges against the unredeemed human being Paul packs into just one verse.

The only way out of this fallen state is Jesus Christ. Those who trust in him are brought from death to life (Rom 6:13). We now have the mind of Christ (1 Cor 2:16).

Paul says we renew our minds so that we can discern the will of God, which is good, acceptable, and perfect (Rom 12:2). The Greek word for *discern* also has the sense of approving or agreeing with what God desires. Once we understand what God wants, we will want to do it, because it is *good* (as God is good), *acceptable* (pleasing to God), and *perfect* (mature). Thus the renewed mind is a moral consciousness that enables us to please God in every circumstance.

Douglas Moo states that the renewed mind has replaced Old Testament law as the believers' guide for conduct, a point that is significant for Paul's argument in Romans. Because Paul taught Jewish converts to Christ that they are no longer under the law (6:14), his Jewish opponents attacked his gospel for promoting lawlessness. So here in 12:2 Paul responds that believers in Christ do not need OT law to tell them what to do.

We now follow "the law of Christ" (Gal 6:2)—everything Jesus and the apostles taught about the will of God. Our renewed minds, instructed by the word of God as illuminated by the Holy Spirit, will guide us in knowing how to please God. Moo says, "Paul's vision, to which he calls us, is of Christians whose minds are so thoroughly renewed that we know from within, almost instinctively, what we are to do to please God in any given situation."[3]

Although we don't need to obey OT law, we do need Scripture (all of it, OT and NT)—to read and study it, and then trust its truth and the Holy Spirit to do their work in our minds and hearts. The word of God sanctifies us (as Jesus prayed in John 17:17) by setting us apart from the world to do God's will. So important is the renewing of our mind by the word that our sanctification will grind to a halt without it. Our new heart and mind crave Scripture.

Now, after a few comments on the nature of sin, we will go on to see what the Bible has to say about resisting sin.

Sin's Deceptive Attraction

All sin, intentional or not, is a violation of our relationship with God. Willful sin is rebellion against the rule of God, but our struggle as believers is generally against sins we do not want to do. Our conversion gave birth to healthy new desires, and then

3. Moo, *Romans*, 758.

we discovered to our dismay that we still have to deal with many of the sinful habits, attitudes, and motivations of our past. New sin patterns, subtle tempters like self-righteousness and pride, also took root.

In the believer, sin continues to feed on a variety of motivations. Some sins rule over us with a power we want to escape but cannot. But what if we enjoy the sin? Is it possible to grieve the loss of sin? Can fear of the unknown keep a person in bondage to sin?

Consider the example of a man in his late twenties with a history of sexual sin. His immoral lifestyle combined with his natural charm to attract young women who were also acting out sexually. Their corresponding, mutually reinforcing sin patterns were bringing spiritual destruction on both him and the women.

Problem was that this young man for years had enjoyed the flirting glances and attention he got from young women. So not many days after repentance and a prayer of deliverance the man began to miss the affirmation from young women and went back to his former lifestyle.

The fellow was candid about it, having told a pastor he saw himself getting older and couldn't let go of his need to know he was still attractive to women. His deliberate choice to sin was less for the physical pleasure than for his need for affirmation.

This example points out the complex motives that can lead to sin. Often the reasons are not evident on the surface, and people may not be fully aware why they do what they do. We need to discern root motives, because in the end the issue will always come down to what a person most of all desires or is trying hard to avoid.

A Christian ministry reaches out to prostitutes, some of whom were forced as children into the sex trade industry. When they are saved out of prostitution and given counseling, food, and a place of safety, a sad thing happens. Some 90 percent of them return to their pimps and prostitution. Why do they do this? It's what they're used to—the way of life that is more familiar to them. They reason it's better to endure the abuse and depravity they know than to enter a future life they do not know.

The prostitutes may believe that God exists. They might think of him as being all-powerful, maybe even loving. Yet we can understand why they wouldn't entrust their future to God if they thought he did not have *their* interests in mind. They need to know that if they trust God who is always good and is *for* them, God will extend favor and blessings far beyond what they could imagine. They need to be convinced there is a better way to live.

A Stronger Power

If we have come to realize that sin in the end hurts others and ourselves, we will more likely have the desire to escape it. But even this desire is not strong enough to overcome sin's attraction. So I suggest that we must deal with sin from a different mindset.

If you have been unable to conquer a particular sin or a lifestyle of sin, I want you to consider a different solution. The biblical way to conquer sin is, first, of course, to confess it and repent of it, and then to overwhelm it with a stronger desire and a stronger power.

In the person of the Holy Spirit, God has indeed blessed us with a source of power to resist sin. But to speak in terms of *resistance* is a negative way to view the Holy Spirit's work. More accurately, the Spirit enables us to resist sin by strengthening our desire *for God*. The Holy Spirit is the stronger power—the "active ingredient" in the process of sanctification—who equips us to conquer the lesser power of sin's attraction by increasing our attraction to God.

Jesus told his disciples he would send the Holy Spirit to convict the world of sin, of righteousness, and of judgment (John 16:8), and J. I. Packer points out that this ministry of the Spirit continues lifelong even for believers: "This threefold conviction is still God's means of making sin repulsive and Christ adorable in the eyes of persons who previously loved sin and cared nothing for the divine Savior."[4]

---

4. Packer, *Concise Theology*, "Illumination."

Let's explore together how we can grow in our adoration of Christ by the enabling power of the Holy Spirit.

Walking by the Spirit

If I had to select one verse that offers the best overall guidance for our role in sanctification, I would choose what Paul says in Galatians 5:16: "But I say, walk by the Spirit, and you will not gratify the desires of the flesh." This is a powerful principle for growth as a Christian. Simply put, the best way to defeat the negative is to run to the positive.

In verse 17 Paul speaks of the war between flesh and Spirit. Maybe this illustration will explain what he means. Say you trade your gasoline-powered car for a new one that runs on diesel. You love your new car, which is "dead" to gasoline. But then you make the mistake of filling the tank with gas, which wages war against your new car's injectors.

Now you must take the car to a mechanic for removal of the gasoline and repair of the damages ("repentance"). You resolve never again to put gas in your car ("serve the flesh") and to always fill the car's tank with diesel ("live by the Spirit"). Just as your car runs smoothly on the correct fuel, you will enjoy life a lot more when you live by the Spirit. This is discipline that works!

In Ephesians 5:18–21 we find the command to be filled with the Spirit. Paul explains what a Spirit-filled life looks like by linking to the verb *filled* five participles: (1) *speaking* to one another in psalms and hymns and spiritual songs, (2 and 3) *singing* and *making melody* in your heart to the Lord, (4) *giving thanks* always for all things to the Father in the name of our Lord Jesus Christ, and (5) *submitting* to one another in the fear of God.

Fellowship with other believers, worship, a thankful heart, and a humble concern for the interests of others invite the Holy Spirit into our lives and make us more alive to God. As we immerse ourselves in these things of the Holy Spirit we will progressively lose interest in the deeds of the flesh. Seek every opportunity to be in the presence of the Spirit: worship services, prayer and devotions, and acts of love and service to others. Ask Spirit-filled people to bless and pray for you. Stop fighting your hunger and eat some food!

Moody's Example

Dwight L. Moody, who lived from 1837 to 1899, has been called the greatest evangelist of the nineteenth century. He founded the Moody Church, several schools, the Moody Bible Institute, and Moody Publishers. Moody described himself as an ordinary man, but one thing he did claim was victory over sin by being filled with the Holy Spirit, a lesson he taught others:

> Moody once illustrated this truth as follows: "Tell me," he said to his audience, "How can I get the air out of this glass?" One man said, "Suck it out with a pump." Moody replied, "That would create a vacuum and shatter the glass." After many impossible suggestions, Moody smiled, picked up a pitcher of water, and filled the glass. "There," he said, "all the air is now removed." He then went on to show that victory in the Christian life is not by "sucking out a sin here and there," but rather by being filled with the Spirit.[5]

When we occupy ourselves with things of the Spirit we have less time for indulgence. In this sense, we overcome evil with good. When we fall in love with Jesus, we fall out of love with the world. When we run to Jesus, we run away from the world and the flesh.

Sowing and Reaping

A related principle is sowing and reaping, a law of God that governs both natural and spiritual realms. What we sow to the flesh versus the Spirit determines what we will reap:

> For the one who sows to his own flesh will from the flesh reap corruption, but the one who sows to the Spirit will

5. Tan, *Encyclopedia.*

> from the Spirit reap eternal life. And let us not grow
> weary of doing good, for in due season we will reap, if we
> do not give up. (Gal 6:7–9)

What kind of harvest do we want? If we want corn, we plant corn seed. If we want love, joy, and peace, we plant things of the Spirit. In the context of Galatians 6, Paul speaks of doing good to others, especially our brothers and sisters in the faith. Service to others is a powerful antidote to two modern diseases of the soul: introspection and the quest for self-fulfillment.

Paul counsels patience. We may have to wait a long time to reap our spiritual harvest, but it will come in due time, so we must persist in doing good and not give up.

Replace Vices with Virtues

Along this same line, the biblical way to overcome a negative habit is to replace it with a positive one. Paul gives some practical examples in Ephesians 4. We stop lying not by taking a vow of silence but by telling the truth (verse 25). The thief stops stealing and does honest work so he can accumulate wealth to share with others (verse 28). We replace gossip and slander with words that encourage and build up others (verse 29).

Many negative emotions likewise can be overcome by positive, proactive thoughts and actions, as in Paul's concluding example: anger and bitterness must give way to kindness, forgiveness, and compassion (verse 32). Jesus said to pray for those who persecute you (Matt 5:44), and in like manner blessing is a great antidote to bitterness.

Are you tempted to jealousy? I recognized a young man's growth in Christlike character when he began praying for the new boyfriend of a young woman who was the object of his own affections. He could have responded to rejection with despair, but instead did what he thought Jesus would do.

Are you prone to depression? I know several people who require treatment for bipolar and other mood disorders that result from chemical imbalance in the brain, and my heart goes out to them. If your depression has been clinically diagnosed, do follow your doctor's advice. Please understand that I do not presume depression is sin or the result of sin.

Some depression, however, can result from a wrong response to circumstances. If that describes you, please consider how you can recast the way you think and feel. Feelings do respond in part to behavior, and if we respond biblically to disappointment and frustrations, peace and joy will more likely follow.

Good things happen when we think and act from the godly impulses of the new heart we received at the moment of our regeneration, as I discussed earlier in this chapter. This new heart rejoices in tribulations (Rom 5:2) and considers it joy to encounter trials (Jas 1:2). We can resign ourselves to unhappiness when things go wrong or we can look at difficulties through the eyes of faith, seeing them as opportunities to persevere, knowing that we will reap full and complete joy.

When James says to *consider* or *count* it all joy when we meet various trials, note the similarity to *reckoning*. James would have us rethink our normal response to difficulties, and Paul in Romans 6:11 would have us rethink our normal response to temptation and sin. Both commands require living in alignment with what God has already done for us. So if our typical response is to bemoan our situation, why not do the opposite: pour out our heart to God and tell Jesus how wise and faithful he is.

Or get even more radical: dance and sing praises, considering ourselves dead to both sin and depression. We will become more alive to God as he turns our mourning into dancing.

There is no better way to conclude this discussion of the principle of replacing vices with virtues than to repeat Paul's admonition in Ephesians 5:18— "And do not get drunk with wine, for that is debauchery, but be filled with the Spirit."

Bottom line: The theme common to all the recommendations in this chapter is that we who believe in Christ are made new in him. Christ set us free to love and serve God.

If sins are the result of a strong desire, then godly conduct is the result of a much stronger desire. The source of that godly desire is our new heart and renewed mind, and the power to realize that desire is the Spirit who indwells us and inspires adoration of Jesus Christ. With God now our reward and the love, joy, and peace of the Spirit our fuel, we gladly let go of lesser pleasures to enjoy his embrace. The greatest of all pleasures is to know that we please God.

7

Paul's Evildoing "I" in Romans 7

D OES THE APOSTLE PAUL, after telling us in Romans 6 to reckon ourselves dead to sin, admit in the next chapter that not even he could resist sin? Taking Paul's words at face value, he does speak pessimistically about his own struggle: "For I do not do the good I want, but the evil I do not want is what I keep on doing" (verse 19).

Interpretation of Romans 7:14–25 has challenged Bible scholars through the ages, and we cannot be certain we understand Paul. Of most relevance for us is whether this passage describes Paul's experience as a Christian. His use of "I" with present-tense verbs has convinced many Bible readers he is describing his own struggle. If the most dedicated Christian of all time cannot escape the bondage of sin, then we must lower our own expectations. But might he be describing something else?

If Romans 7 is a self-portrait, Paul would seem unable to obey his own command not to let "sin therefore reign in your mortal body, to make you obey its passions" (6:12). And how could he describe himself in 7:14 as "sold under sin" (an image of slavery) after telling his readers in chapter 6 that they have been set free from slavery to sin?

Those who want to take Paul's wording at face value and say it describes his Christian experience cannot avoid softening the force of the text. But Paul's language does not allow degrees of sinfulness or mixing of desires. The text, as in verse 19, expresses uniformity of both desire (to do good) and outcome (to practice evil). The Paul we know from the rest of Scripture hardly corresponds with someone who is unable to do what is right and keeps on doing what is evil.

Paul the Rhetorician

Some Romans scholars, unable to reconcile the "I" in chapter 7 with Paul's description of the Christian life in chapters 6 and 8, are persuaded that Paul is not writing about himself at all, either before or after his conversion. He might be using a dramatic figure of speech to make a point about sin and the law. If so, this chapter is an example of Paul's sophisticated rhetoric, which is also how some early church fathers saw the chapter.

One clue clearly stands out. From verse 14 to the end of that chapter Paul repeats the personal pronouns "I" and "me" some thirty times and refers not a single time to the Holy Spirit. In chapter 8, as Paul reverts to the normal, direct style of his epistles, we find the opposite: a single use of *me* in the first seventeen verses and fifteen references to the Holy Spirit. Now Paul speaks of *those* who live according to the flesh. Paul does not associate himself with carnality, because he finds his identity in Christ, who through the cross put to death the old self of sin. Paul now walks by the power of the Holy Spirit, set free from the law of sin and death. So the identity Paul assigns to the "I" in chapter 7 appears to differ from his normal voice in chapter 8.

In Paul's day, speakers and writers sought to persuade their audiences with a variety of rhetorical devices, and Paul was a master of this ancient art of persuasion, says Ben Witherington III in his guidebook on New Testament rhetoric. He is one of many current scholars who believe chapter 7 showcases Paul's use of "impersonation," also known as speech-in-character. The speaker or writer uses a change of voice, in this case the introduction of "I," to clue the audience he is taking on another character's role.

Identifying the "I"

What individual or group of people was Paul impersonating? Several options present themselves, and scholars exercise their own art of persuasion in making the case for ones they prefer. I will cite four.

In his 2012 Romans commentary, Colin G. Kruse notes growing support for the view that the "I" denotes the experience of Israel as a nation. He points to the significance of Paul's shift from the past (aorist) tense in 7:7–13 to the present tense in 7:14–25. The "I" in the former passage, Kruse says, refers to Israel's historical, failed encounter with the law given at Sinai, and in the latter passage the "I" represents Israel's current experience of living under the law.

This view, Kruse says, "has the advantage not only of recognizing that Paul is adopting the rhetorical device of speech-in-character (*prosopopoeia*) . . . but also of recognizing the fact that it is the encounter of the 'I' with the Mosaic law that is described in this passage."[1] Kruse notes that this portrait draws in part from Paul's own pre-Christian experience. He emphasizes that the problem is not the law, but human sin: "Paul firmly locates the root cause of the human dilemma with sin, not the law, and by so doing rejects all suggestions that his gospel involves a denigration of the law."[2]

A similar view is offered by Douglas Moo, who concluded in his 1996 commentary that Paul speaks of himself in solidarity with the Jewish people. The "I" is a representative Jew living under the Mosaic law, Moo concludes.

Another option, presented well by Witherington, is that Paul has in mind Adam's sin. Paul has already spoken in chapter 5 about Adam as a representative of humanity in that his sin brought death upon the entire race. Witherington says Paul expands on that narrative in chapter 7, now telling "the story of Adam from the past in vv. 7–13, and the story of all those in Adam in the present in vv.

1. Kruse, *Romans*, 320.
2. Ibid., 312.

14–25."[3] The "I" in the latter part of the chapter, then, represents more broadly the bondage of all unredeemed humanity—Jews and Gentiles alike—to sin and death, Witherington says. The only way a person can escape this plight is to move from being "in Adam" to being "in Christ," and thus to walk in the newness of life Paul will describe in chapter 8.

Kruse, who also recognizes Paul's allusions to Adam in the passage, regards "Israel's encounter with the law a recapitulation of Adam's encounter with the commandment in Eden."[4] Moo, in 2012 lectures[5] on Romans, says he now thinks more highly of the Adam view than he did when he wrote his commentary.

For the fourth view, Richard N. Longenecker is author of the most recent scholarly commentary on Romans. Recognizing the speech-in-character rhetorical form of the passage, Longenecker aligns in some respects with the Adam view without specifically mentioning it. He thinks Paul does not speak of his own experience or that of a representative Jew, but rather of "the tragic plight of all people who attempt to live their lives by their own natural abilities and acquired resources, apart from God."[6] Spiritually sensitive pagans, for example, are aware of what is good and right but often do evil and wrong. Paul's "awful lament" about the human predicament prepares unbelievers for the gospel message of chapter 8 and teaches Christians to rely on the ministry of the Spirit, Longenecker concludes.

Interpretation of Romans 7 remains a challenge, but we can be thankful that scholars of this epistle continue to gain insight.

Christ's Knockout Blow to Sin

We find a clue to at least a significant part of the puzzle of chapter 7 in Romans 8:3. There Paul speaks of the law as powerless in the

---

3. Witherington, *New Testament Rhetoric*, 145.

4. Kruse, *Romans*, 320.

5. www.biblicaltraining.org.

6. Longenecker, *Romans*, 673.

sense that, while perfect in itself, the law was "weakened" by sin, which prevents obedience to the law's requirements.

Picture a boxing match between law and sin. Sin will always win, because no law—even God's "holy and righteous and good" commandment (7:12)—is strong enough to stand up against the brute force of sin in the human heart. Paul's gift to us in chapter 7 is to prove how weak and useless the law is to deliver us from bondage to sin.

We are thankful the story does not end in chapter 7, because the next chapter tells of a new law that delivered a knockout blow to sin. What even the divinely conceived Mosaic law could not do, or certainly any human-made law, rule, resolution, or vow could not do, God did by instituting a new law: "For the law of the Spirit of life has set you free in Christ Jesus from the law of sin and death" (8:2). This new law is the liberating power of the Holy Spirit dwelling in every believer.

Of course, it took the sacrificial work of a sinless Man to bring this law into existence. Jesus entered the ring and fought on our behalf, taking on himself the condemnation for our sin. For this reason, the law of the Spirit is operative only for those who are "in Christ Jesus." As Paul says in verse 1, "There is therefore now no condemnation for those who are in Christ Jesus."

The redeemed Jews and Gentiles in Rome who gathered to hear this new letter from Paul could see in their own past the confirmation of these truths about law and sin, and Paul wants them to know they have been delivered. Imagine the cheer going up when they heard the dramatic and joyful conclusion: "Thanks be to God through Jesus Christ our Lord!"

Confronting Sin with Confidence

One thing we can be sure about is that Romans 7 offers no rationale to resign ourselves to sin. At one time or another, however, we can relate to Paul's anguishing statement in verse 15: "For I do not do what I want, but I do the very thing I hate." Even Spirit-empowered believers at times can feel as helpless as Paul's rhetorical "I" to abstain from sin's temptations.

Other Bible passages describe the very real battle between flesh and Spirit each Christian faces, and we have looked at several of them with our focus on those that point the way to victory. We can expect *relative* victory—never free of sin's temptations, but not having to yield to them—when we deal with sin the biblical way.

Paul in all his letters presents an optimistic view of sanctification that both comforts and challenges us to live not as frustrated sinners but in accord with our new identity in Christ as regenerated, righteous, victorious people. Consider, for example, how Paul addresses the believers in Corinth in this passage:

> Or do you not know that the unrighteous will not inherit the kingdom of God? Do not be deceived: neither the sexually immoral, nor idolaters, nor adulterers, nor men who practice homosexuality, nor thieves, nor the greedy, nor drunkards, nor revilers, nor swindlers will inherit the kingdom of God. (1 Cor 6:9–10)

After listing these types of sinners, Paul adds, "And such were some of you." Note the past tense. Failure to conquer such sins was unthinkable to Paul, who settled for nothing less than victory through Christ. Thus he assures the Corinthians of their present standing: "But you were washed, you were sanctified, you were justified in the name of the Lord Jesus Christ and by the Spirit of our God" (verse 11). Now declared righteous and progressively being cleansed of their former sinful lifestyles by the sanctifying work of the Holy Spirit, they were able to live righteously by the power of the Holy Spirit.

We too were washed, sanctified, and justified in the name of our Lord Jesus Christ and by the Spirit of our God. We too can live righteously by the power of the Holy Spirit.

8

Calling Things That Are Not as Though They Were

Not only is Abraham the father of faith, he is the father of reckoning. We can better understand the close relationship between faith and reckoning by looking at these themes in the life of Abraham. It is in Paul's reference to Abraham in chapter 4 of Romans that we find the apostle's first use of reckoning, though with a different twist than we have seen in chapter 6.

In chapter 4, verse 9, while making his case for justification by faith, Paul says faith was "counted" to Abraham as righteousness. The Greek word for *counted* (ESV; NASB reads *credited*) is the same word we find in 6:11 *(reckoned)*. The difference between here and chapter 6 is the actor. Here reckoning is God's action, not Abraham's. But Abraham responded to God's initiative with his own reckoning, as we will see more clearly below.

So the meaning is this: because of Abraham's faith, God credited righteousness into Abraham's account. Thereafter, Abraham could count, consider, or *reckon* himself to be righteous.

The Childless Father of Many Nations

The window opens wider on the role of reckoning in Abraham's life in verse 17 of chapter 4. There Paul quotes God's declaration to Abraham in Genesis 17:5: "I have made you a father of many nations." Note the past tense. In God's eyes, Abraham was already the father of many nations, even though at this time Abraham was still childless.

Sarah had not yet given birth to Isaac, yet God was speaking as if Isaac, Jacob, and all future generations—descendants so plentiful as to constitute many nations—already existed. For this reason Paul goes on in this verse to say that God "calls those things which do not exist as though they did" (NKJ) or, as ESV translates, "calls into existence the things that do not exist."[1]

Because of what God said, now Abraham was entitled to say the same thing—calling himself a father of many nations. We know from reading Genesis that it took a while for Abraham to come around to this level of faith. Eventually he did, and Paul declares that Abraham became fully convinced that God was able to perform what he had promised (verse 21). Then in verse 22 Paul repeats the vital truth of verse 9: "it was accounted to him for righteousness."

When God changed Abraham's name from Abram ("exalted father") to Abraham ("father of a multitude"), Isaac's birth was still twenty-five years away. Yet whenever someone asked Abraham for his name, he couldn't respond without calling something that was not as though it were. People may well have laughed at him, just as people may laugh at us today for saying God calls us righteous, but God honored Abraham by holding him up as the father of faith for all of us who believe.

---

1. In the context, this rendering is probably correct, as it highlights God's creative declaration establishing a new reality for Abraham. Although Abraham continues to live in the old reality and does not yet see the evidence of this new reality, he will from this time increasingly orient his speech and actions to the new reality. On the basis of his faith in God's promise, God credits righteousness to Abraham's account. Now it is Abraham himself, in an ironic twist on the NKJ wording, who is able to call those things that do not exist as though they did.

Faith That Releases God's Creative Power

Even though in verse 17 it is God who brings something into being from nothing, in a limited sense it is also true that our faith in God's promises can bring some things into being that wouldn't otherwise exist. If that were not the case, there would be no reason to pray. Our faith releases God's creative power in our lives and the lives of those for whom we pray.

Notice what Jesus told us to do to receive answers to our prayers: "Therefore I say to you, whatever things you ask when you pray, believe that you receive them, and you will have them" (Mark 11:24). When we pray for something, our confidence in God's provision should be so high as to believe we already possess what we ask for. The clear implication is that we would not have certain things unless we ask and believe as though we already have them.

Calling things that are not as though they were is another way to describe reckoning. How do we conquer sin? We insist and declare over ourselves that our old self was crucified with Christ even when the evidence clearly suggests otherwise, when the old self still seems way too much alive.

This is the kind of faith, when we persist in it, that conquers sin. Paul was not using sarcasm when he addressed the Corinthian believers as "saints" even though their behavior was in a lot of ways carnal. He was calling them to live up to their true identity as a holy people set apart for God.

Living by Faith in the "Not yet"

As discussed in the previous chapters, seeing ourselves as God sees us has the power to change our lives. Ponder the prayers of the Apostle Paul in chapters 1 and 3 in Ephesians. God wants us to know the hope of his calling and the greatness of his power toward us. He wants us to comprehend his love which surpasses knowledge. He tells us to be mindful of our position in the heavenly places in Christ. He wants us to see ourselves as his adopted sons clothed with Christ.

Blessings such as these are legal entitlements of the New Covenant. God has given us the Holy Spirit as a pledge or down payment (2 Cor 5:1–5), but we do not yet enjoy full possession of these blessings. Theologians speak of the New Covenant as inaugurated but not yet consummated. We enjoy some of its blessings in the "already," while others remain in the realm of "not yet."

I find in Mark's Gospel reason to believe God delights when we chase after every blessing possible, maybe even some that are "not yet." Mark tells of a Gentile woman who asked Jesus to cast a demon out of her daughter (7:25–30). Jesus denied her request with picturesque language that conveyed a blunt and unmistakable message: his ministry at that time was for the Jews first and Gentiles would have to wait. But she would not go away. When she persisted in asking for a blessing that was not yet rightfully hers, Jesus granted her request. The demon left her daughter instantly.

Of course, Jesus all the while was testing the woman's faith to see how hard she would push against the barrier of Jesus' ministry to Gentiles at that stage of salvation history. We get the sense that he was delighted to lose an argument to a woman of such great faith and insight into the ways of God. This woman was spiritually informed. She knew the merciful heart of God and also was aware that a time was coming when God would open the door of blessing to Gentiles. Why not bring that future into her present for the deliverance of her daughter!

God is both willing and able "to do far more abundantly than all that we ask or think, according to the power at work within us" (Eph 3:20).

Transforming Our "Already"

As we ponder God's promises and his wonder-working power, our faith will grow and we will begin to see a transformation in our "already." In this regard we have much in common with Abraham, who dwelt in a foreign country yet regarded it as the land of promise. He regarded land that was not yet his as though it were his. He and the other heroes of faith mentioned in Hebrews 11 ordered their thoughts and actions as though the promises were more real than what they saw with their eyes. Faith inspired their works of self-sacrifice.

Like them, we shrug off suffering and hardship, giving more attention to the glory that awaits us. Faith and hope increase. We begin to see growth of Christlike character.

The challenge for us, as it was for those who have gone before us, is to steadfastly exercise our faith while we live in the incomplete "already" where so much of sin and Satan and sickness remain. Why not push back against these evils, because even now they have no right to afflict us because of Christ's victory over them.

By faith we can lay hold of many more of the blessings already available to us in the present expression of God's kingdom, and we might even be able to draw some of the "not yet" into our "already."

Authentic faith is not passive but active. And that is why it's so important to know that our speech—what we say, what we call things, who we declare ourselves to be—must come into alignment with God's promises. "Death and life are in the power of the tongue, and those who love it will eat its fruit" (Prov 18:21). This proverb is a warning about the use of our tongue; let's be careful to speak words that bear good fruit.

We avoid both "God will do what God will do" passivity and "name it and claim it" presumption. When we actively call (or count, consider, *reckon*) those good and godly things that are not yet in our experience as though they were, we set ourselves along a path to enjoy a more fruitful life of service to our Lord.

9

Now Enforce the Word of God in Your Life

A T THE RISK OF seeming to finish this part of the book with a pep talk, I want to emphasize the previous chapter's concluding point about the need to avoid passivity. This chapter encourages you to be ruthless in your fight against sin, and it offers a reminder of why you fight.

On Patrol against Lawlessness

In the old West, a frontier town was fortunate to have a strong and competent marshal to keep the peace. The marshal had to know how to handle a gun and he also had to have the courage and no-nonsense attitude to be able to round up cattle rustlers and horse thieves and sometimes duke it out with them and other outlaws. A town would be ill served by a lawman who sought to avoid confrontation by kicking back in the office all day with heels planted on his desk.

Just as passivity was not part of the job description for a marshal, it will not do for a Christian. Sin crouches at the door, the Lord told Cain. "Its desire is for you, but you must rule over it" (Gen 4:7). As we know, Cain's anger got the best of him and he killed his brother Abel. Sin wants to rule over you as well, but now sin is a defeated foe, put to death by Jesus Christ on the cross.

As Paul explains in Romans 6, you have been set free from sin by having died and been buried with Christ, so sin no longer has the right nor power to dominate you. Yet sin crouches at the door of your heart as it did Cain's, and it would lure and entice you to succumb to its desire (Jas 1:14–15). Maybe sin has busted through the door of your heart so many times that you despair of ever enjoying the victory that is rightfully yours.

I hope you will not give up. God has done his part to provide everything you need for victory, as the previous chapters explain. You have a part to play as well, and now I draw attention to one key responsibility: you must enforce the word of God in your life.

When a marshal arrives in a lawless town, he shows his badge and goes on the offense, letting everyone know the limits of the law. He patrols the town, shotgun in hand, and rounds up lawbreakers. You wear the badge of Christ's authority and now patrol your heart to round up everything that violates the will of God in your life.

I'm pushing the metaphor to its limits, but this is roughly what it means to enforce the word of God in your life. With courage and a no-nonsense attitude, you must confront lawlessness in thought, word, and deed with the sword of the Spirit, the word of God. You must reckon yourself dead to all that does not align with God's word and insist that you will have the victory through Christ. You are enforcing "the law of the Spirit of life" that has "set you free in Christ Jesus from the law of sin and death" (Rom 8:2).

In It to Win It

Jesus spoke fighting words. He said he did not come to bring peace but a sword (Matt 10:34), and he warned that "whoever does not take his cross and follow me is not worthy of me" (10:38). Passive disciples will fall behind as Jesus pushes forward in his offensive against all that opposes his kingdom. Those who look back after putting their hand to the plow are not fit for his kingdom (Luke 9:62).

Paul chose military and athletic metaphors to describe Christian service, and he referred to those serving with him as "fellow soldiers" (Phil 2:25; Phlm 2). Believers must be strong in the Lord and put on their spiritual armor (Eph 6:1–2).

To enforce the word of God against sin is to enforce the reality that in Christ you died to sin and it no longer has dominion over you (Rom 6:7). You are insisting that your experience come into alignment with what God accomplished for you on the cross.

Passivity will not win this war. Confess every particular sin, proclaim your victory in Christ over the sin, and use your command voice in the name of Christ against any stronghold of sin just as you would when dealing with an unruly animal. Avoid passive praying where you tell God what he already knows and endlessly rehearse the problem.

I once had a worrisome infection on my skin. When I asked my doctor what he would do about it, he said, "I'll kill it." I love that ruthless attitude, and his response gave confidence I would soon be well. The psalmist had this same attitude: "All nations surrounded me; in the name of the LORD I cut them off!" (Ps 118:10).

No need to wonder if it is God's will to set you free. The word of God makes that clear. It *is* his will. So if you truly want to be set free, you will win this fight. Jesus has done everything necessary to set you free (John 8:36). Whatever thing stands in the way of your freedom to live righteously—anger, lust, addiction, greed, gluttony, pride, unforgiveness—cut it off in the all-powerful name of Jesus Christ!

Testimonial by J. I. Packer

Few people have modeled love for the word of God more than Dr. Packer, who retired in 2003 as Professor of Systematic and Historical Theology at Regent College. Packer converted to Christianity in his late teens. "I had kept Christ at bay for too long and was trying to make up for lost time. Like any other introverted adolescent, I was a loner, my emotional life was all over the place, and I was essentially a mixed-up kid."[1] Packer describes his struggle against sin as a young believer:

> Now that I was a regenerate believer, born again, a new creation in Christ, sin that formerly dominated me had been dethroned but was not yet destroyed. It was marauding within me all the time, bringing back sinful desires that I hoped I had seen the last of, and twisting my new desires for God and godliness out of shape so that they became pride-perverted too.[2]

Packer first listened to preachers of the "Victorious Spirit-filled life" who taught that if you make a total surrender to Jesus Christ, he would "douse the desire" of sinful urges when you looked to him. Striving hard for deeper consecration, Packer couldn't get this method to work. He then turned to the Puritan writer John Owen, whose work *Of the Mortification of Sin in Believers* exposed Packer to the "egocentric energy" of sin in his heart. Packer summarizes the essence of Owen's answer to the problem of sin:

> Have the holiness of God clear in your mind. Remember that sin desensitizes you to itself. Watch, that is, prepare to recognize it, and search it out within you by disciplined, Bible-based, Spirit-led self-examination. Focus on the living Christ and his love for you on the cross. Pray, asking for strength to say "no" to sin's suggestions and to fortify yourself against bad habits by forming good ones contrary to them. And ask Christ to kill the sinful urge you are fighting.[3]

Dr. Packer expresses many of the principles featured in this book: search-and-destroy mission against sin, discipline,

---

1. Packer, *Christian History.*
2. Ibid.
3. Ibid.

dependence on the Bible as guide and Spirit for power, thirst for Christ's love, and replacement of vices with virtues.

Christian repentance begins with an admission that we have sinned and a willingness to surrender to the will of God. But passive mental assent, no matter how deep our consecration or total our surrender, will not get the job done. To repent is to join the fight alongside Jesus against everything in us that opposes his rule.

Jesus the Warrior-Messiah

Perhaps we will be more motivated to deal with sin if we catch a glimpse of the raging fire in Jesus' soul as he began his march to the cross. Jesus Christ is the Marshal of the universe. When rebellion broke the tranquility of Eden, the divine plan was already set for this Marshal to set foot on earth and restore order. Jesus came with a fiery resolve to set the captives free from sin and death.

Several events have brought tears to my eyes over the years, but nothing quite like when my mother died. I cried for nearly an entire day and then at times for many days after. When I last saw her in our living room she was the picture of health, then a couple days later she was gone. It is impossible to be indifferent to the death of someone we love.

We "groan inwardly," as Paul says in Romans 8, over the sufferings of this present time, chief among which is death. Jesus wept at the tomb of Lazarus. But his tears revealed only part of his intensely emotional response to the death of his friend. He also *groaned,* and that word, as I will show you, does not come close to describing the depth of Jesus' feelings.

In John 11:33 we find striking insight into the emotional life of our Lord. Jesus arrives on the scene and finds Mary and her friends *wailing.* That Greek word, *klaiousan,* expresses audible wailing and weeping. Loud lamenting of this kind was the customary response of Middle Eastern mourners at a funeral. The response of Jesus, on the other hand, was quite unlike any ordinary human custom.

The Lord's Fiery Indignation

Having noted the crowd's wailing, John then says of Jesus that he *groaned* in the spirit. This New King James translation of a Greek word is unfortunately weak and leaves us wanting to know what kind of groan this was. Both the Message Bible and the New Living Translation, not usually esteemed for textual accuracy, are much more on target: *"a deep anger welled up within him."* NASB renders it *"deeply moved in spirit"* and ESV is similar.

This Greek word, in verse 33 and repeated in 38, is *enebrime-sato* and literally means to snort like a horse. Picture a warhorse, nostrils flaring, eager for the charge. The word means to be angry, to shudder, to be moved with indignation, to express fiery indignation, to be enraged. This was a groan of outrage!

B.B. Warfield studied the meaning of this word and concluded, "What John tells us, in point of fact, is that Jesus approached the grave of Lazarus, in a state, not of uncontrollable grief, but of irrepressible anger."[4]

It is likely we encounter in this scene and in this word the temperament of the Warrior-Messiah who is described in Revelation 19. The difference is that when Jesus walked up to the grave of Lazarus he expressed his intense anger at death in a groan discernible only by those nearby. But that same anger will be in full display for all on this planet to see when he later returns to judge and make war against everything opposed to the rule of God. We will ride with him and, being then fully conformed to his image, we will share the fullness of his wrath at the enemies of our King.

The righteous anger of Jesus at the grave of his friend fueled his march to the cross, where he would pay the price of his own death to conquer sin and death and to destroy the power of the devil, the murderer of humanity. His loud cry "Lazarus, come forth!" was a command that death release one of its captives and a foretelling of his own victorious resurrection, and of ours.

Now that you understand Jesus' righteous anger against all that opposes the rule of God, you have all the more resolve to wage

4. Warfield, *Emotional Life of Our Lord*, II.

war against the sin in your own life. He fought on your behalf with the price of his death so that you might reckon yourself dead to sin. He lives now to fight alongside you so you can live in the freedom he has already won for you.

"You who love the LORD, hate evil!" (Ps 97:10).

Pleasing the Lord Who Loves Us

Finally, keep in mind the purpose of all your effort. Here it is in Paul's advice to one of his young lieutenants: "No soldier gets entangled in civilian pursuits, since his aim is to please the one who enlisted him" (2 Tim 2:4). Pleasing your Lord—aligning your desire with his holy purpose—is your motivation and inspiration for fighting alongside him.

Obedience is the fruit of love. In this light, Jesus' statement to his disciples in John 14:15—"If you love me you will keep my commandments"—is not a question with an uncertain outcome but a statement of probability. The more you love Jesus, the more you will fight to obey him and to be like him.

With confidence in God's love for us, we surrender our desire to his desire, and make his desire our desire. In chapter 15 a young believer named Cody will come to this life-changing realization. Now let us learn from Cody's struggle and victory.

PART 4

Reckoning Illustrated
The Cody Chronicles

THE NEXT SIX CHAPTERS present the life experience of Cody, a young man who transitions from a troubled past to a new life of freedom in Christ by putting into practice the biblical principle of reckoning.

Cody professes faith in Christ and joins a church, but he returns to his former lifestyle. Then, with the guidance of a pastoral counselor, Cody repents, discovers his identity in Christ, breaks the stronghold of bitterness, learns to flex his will by taking ruthless action against sin, and acquires the motivation to please God.

Cody's spiritual transformation may seem unrealistically rapid, and relative to my own many years of ups and downs, his does progress at light-speed. But there is no limit on the pace of our spiritual growth, and certainly no biblical reason why a Christian must endure years of struggle against strongholds of besetting sin.

Why can't a new believer, with good understanding of Scripture and a desire to please God, quickly escape the domination of sin? As Cody did, so can you, by God's amazing grace.

"My brothers, if anyone among you wanders from the truth and someone brings him back, let him know that whoever brings back a sinner from his wandering will save his soul from death and will cover a multitude of sins." (Jas 5:19–20)

10

A Thief Gets Saved

Now let's see how the issues of sin, faith, repentance, and discipleship work out in the life of one young man. I introduce to you Cody, who as a teenager became very good at stealing. Before I tell you what Cody is doing now at age twenty-four, we need to go back in time a few years.

The Quest to Succeed

Cody took well to being a thief. He quit school when he was fifteen and spent most of his time at a downtown park. It was there he met three other dropouts his age. One of them, already an experienced thief, taught the others. Soon Cody, bright and quick-witted, began to excel above them all. Every trick gave him a rush of adrenaline that became addicting.

Cody enjoyed legend status among his fellow thieves, who looked up to him as their leader and role model. Stealing fed both his mouth and his ego. It was Cody's identity.

There was more to Cody than his proficiency as a thief. He valued loyalty to his friends and entertained them with his voice and guitar. But his playful exterior covered a feeling of emptiness, and he would often get alone to think and console himself. He carried bitterness toward his father, who told Cody when he was eleven, "You can't do anything right, you're useless as a broken shoestring and you'll never amount to anything." His parents by then had already separated, and they divorced when he was twelve.

Before he learned to be a successful thief, Cody at age fourteen discovered something else he was good at: sex, after being pursued by a seventeen-year-old neighbor girl. Girls also became a source of alcohol, pot, and occasional drugs.

A Divine Encounter

When he was nineteen, Cody encountered a Christian man handing out sandwiches at the park. This man started a lighthearted conversation with Cody and upon mentioning the Bible sensed that the young man had a softness of heart toward things of God. Cody was indeed ready for something new and felt drawn to the joy and confidence of his new friend.

When a week later the man asked Cody if he would like to place his trust in Jesus Christ, Cody agreed. Though a bit hesitant and not completely understanding what this new life would be like, he prayed the sinner's prayer.

Cody felt a heaviness lift from him, and from that time on he pursued his new life as a Christian. He met frequently with his older friend, got a part-time job, and attended church, where he was welcomed into a fellowship group. Never an avid reader, he found that he did like reading about Jesus in the Gospels.

As the months went by, though, Cody began to find his new routines a bit boring. Church and Bible and small-group meetings, along with part-time work as a cook, still filled his time, but other things began to fill his mind.

Recalling the Pleasures of His past

Alone one night he recalled the exhilaration of his former life—memories of the thrill of the break-in, his heart racing as he crawled through a window and searched room to room.

Feeling the pull of his former life, Cody thought to himself, "Is this Christian thing really for me? I don't feel any different inside anymore, and I'm not seeing my life change for the better. It felt good at first but now it's a struggle." Lust was consuming him, as everywhere he went girls sought his attention.

Cody especially missed the camaraderie of his downtown mall crew, and he remembered having more fun hanging out with them than with the people at church. Memories and thoughts increasingly turned into intentions, his mind rehearsing the details of the classic robbery.

Three days after his twenty-second birthday Cody was out for a run when he saw one of his former friends, who told him of a heist that was being planned. Would he join them, his friend asked? To pull this one off, his friend insisted, they could really use Cody's help. Without thinking, Cody said, "I'm in."

The little gang had progressed beyond house break-ins; now they were targeting a restaurant, having heard from a guy who had worked there that the owner kept a lot of money in the building. The guy knew the hiding place. They would hit it an hour or so after the restaurant closed that night.

His father's words echoed in Cody's mind. He thought to himself that it must be true: "I'll never change; I'll always be this way; there's no use trying anymore."

What we think we are good at and get rewarded for convinces us that is what we are.

Cody was arrested that night.

Cody is about to enter a new realm in his walk with God. What happens to him next depends on what he reckons to be true—about God, about himself and his destiny.

Cody has fallen, but he did not know that he has fallen right into the arms of Jesus.

11

Cody Repents

"Through the LORD's mercies we are not consumed,
Because His compassions fail not.
They are new every morning;
Great is Your faithfulness.
'The LORD is my portion,' says my soul,
'Therefore I hope in Him!'

The LORD is good to those who wait for Him,
To the soul who seeks Him.
It is good that one should hope and wait quietly
For the salvation of the LORD.
It is good for a man to bear
The yoke in his youth.

Let him sit alone and keep silent,
Because God has laid it on him;
Let him put his mouth in the dust—
There may yet be hope."

(LAM 3:22–29 NKJ)

A YOUNG MAN FROM A rough background, saved through a street ministry, initially enthused to follow Jesus then suddenly reverting to his former lifestyle—nothing all that unique. Lonny had seen that pattern play out many times in his inmate-counseling ministry. He had been coming to the jail most Thursday afternoons for the past fifteen years, and he remembers having had little success with these guys during those first few years.

Now something was different. The Lord had given him wisdom and anointing he did not have early on. It wasn't that every inmate he counseled surrendered his life to Jesus and his life turned around. Even now, only a few fit that description.

What was different was that Lonny now could see more quickly the Holy Spirit's working. He knew when to lock in on a young man's heart and when to move on so as not to waste his own and the inmate's time.

This encounter was going to be different for another reason: he and Cody were from the same church. It was a friend of Lonny's who had first shared Christ with Cody, and Lonny was familiar with the teaching and discipleship Cody had received during his couple of years at the church.

Lonny also knew some of the details of Cody's prior life and, as a member of the leadership team, was aware of Cody's declining attendance during the months leading up to his arrest. He had been praying regularly for this young man for what seemed nearly a year now.

"What Do You Want to Do?"

That was the question Lonny intended to ask Cody from the very beginning of their conversations. He had been hopeful Cody's conscience would have kicked in and the young man would have begun his spiritual rebound. Lonny was a bit disappointed and decided he had to move slowly. Not until their third session, after Lonny felt he knew well enough Cody's thought process, did he think it the right time to pose this simple yet fateful question.

Lonny opened his Bible to John 1 and showed Cody verses 37 and 38. Two men who were disciples of John heard their master praise Jesus and say he is the Son of God. So when Jesus came nearby, they took the opportunity to change their allegiance and they began to follow Jesus instead of John. Looking at them, Jesus asked, "What do you seek?"

"What do I seek?" Cody, now twenty-three, had read this passage several times since his confession of Christ four years ago, but he had never pondered its relevance to him. Having spent the last year and a half in prison, this was now the question of his life—an issue of motive and will and faith—and his answer would decide his destiny. But in Cody's mind, he had already tried to follow Jesus and had failed. Here he was in jail having to answer this question only because he had turned back to stealing, something he had been really good at, and had got caught.

Getting caught really wasn't his fault, he told Lonny; it was because of bad intel. The guy they depended on hadn't got his facts straight.

Lonny knew Cody's thinking errors (blaming his partner, etc.), but he would deal with those later. First, he had to ascertain, and try to guide, the allegiance of Cody's heart. Above all else, will Cody love Jesus?

Jesus doesn't compel allegiance; he invites it. Lonny wanted Cody to understand that he was free to choose between God's way and his way. What he wasn't free to choose were the consequences of a bad choice. Those were up to God.

To reinforce this point, Lonny took Cody to Revelation 22:11, where the angel tells John, "Let the evildoer still do evil, and the filthy still be filthy, and the righteous still do right, and the holy still be holy." This is one of Lonny's favorite passages for both evangelism and discipleship, because it warns people they are making a choice by what they do. Their actions confirm their destinies.

In verses 12 and 13 it is Jesus who speaks: "Behold, I am coming soon, bringing my recompense with me, to repay each one for what he has done. I am the Alpha and the Omega, the first and the last, the beginning and the end."

Lonny pressed the question: "What do you want to do with your life now? If you want to do things God's way, I pledge to be here by your side as long as you need me."

Cody appeared to take the question seriously, yet Lonny also sensed resistance. Cody was not yet to the point of deciding. The hour was up for this week, so Lonny encouraged his young friend to think it over and they would continue talking next week.

Trust in the Goodness of God Leads to Repentance

While praying for Cody during the week, Lonny sensed Cody's need for trust in God's goodness. He had to be convinced that God is good, that God is *for* him. So when they met again he used Scripture and illustrations to build Cody's confidence that God will take care of him and give him a future he never thought possible.

Cody had to come to the point of believing that God's "future grace" will satisfy him so completely that he will be willing to surrender now to God's will for his life.

Trust and hope had to come first; otherwise Cody would have no desire to come clean with God. Lonny explained that the next step would be repentance. For some reason neither one of them could explain later, at the mere mention of that word *repentance*, Cody immediately bent forward, sobbing. The sincerity of Cody's outpouring and the softening of his heart were obvious; the kid wasn't feigning his sorrow.

But Lonny knew that repentance is more than emotion. He wanted to see a "yes" form in Cody's heart—yes to the love of Jesus, yes to God's will, yes to whatever it takes. Lonny used the next two sessions to take Cody deeper into an understanding of repentance.

He explained that the word *repentance* means a changing of one's mind, coming to a new way of thinking. He read to Cody a definition he carried with him: "the change of mind of those who have begun to abhor their errors and misdeeds, and have determined to enter upon a better course of life, so that it embraces both a recognition of sin and sorrow for it and hearty amendment, the tokens and effects of which are good deeds."

"We've got to come to the point where we abhor our sin. We've got to hate it," Lonny proclaimed. Then he chuckled as he repeated the old-fashioned phrase "hearty amendment." They laughed together, repeating the words with each different example they could think of. Cody gleefully announced, "Here's my hearty amendment—I kyped this guy's cigarettes. He knows. I'll give him what's left of this pack when I get back inside!" Lonny high-fived him.

A Sin of Omission

Lonny, saying he wanted to make sure Cody understood something else about sin, looked up a verse in 1 John: "No one born of God makes a practice of sinning, for God's seed abides in him, and he cannot keep on sinning because he has been born of God" (3:9).

Lonny explained: "John here is contrasting the children of God with the children of the devil. They carry on sinning as a way of life. That's why John says this in verse 8: 'Whoever makes a practice of sinning is of the devil, for the devil has been sinning from the beginning.'

"We who are born of God want to live by his standard of righteousness. That's our family's DNA, and if we practice the opposite it only shows that we are not his children. See also that John is using present tense—he's talking about a lifestyle.

"And that's not all we need to learn from what John is saying here. John considers righteousness to be not just avoiding specifics sins—you know, don't do this and don't do that—but he is really concerned about loving our brothers and sisters. That's what shows we are born of God. The test of our righteousness is that we love others as he does.

"We show that we have taken on God's character when we love our brothers and sisters, and of course we've got to really do it, not just with sentimental feelings but by acts of love."

Why Do We Have to Live God's Way?

They were quiet for a moment, and then Cody had a question. "I see that God doesn't just let us do our thing. He wants us to do it his way, and I get that because he's God and we're not. But why does God insist on this—you know, why does he want us to behave a certain way? I really don't want to do my own thing anymore. I want to do it his way. I just want to know *why* he wants me to do it his way."

Lonny knew how he would respond, but there wasn't enough time left to say it. "I've got a lot to tell you about this, but it's going to have to wait. I want you to know you have hit upon a super important topic. You have a Bible in your room. Check out Ephesians—the whole six chapters, and we'll talk about this soon."

Lonny hugged Cody and prayed for him, then motioned goodbye when the deputy opened the door. It was a very gratifying feeling knowing that Cody was making significant progress. He thought of a Kim Clement song where Jesus says, "Someone's falling, someone's falling right into my arms." Lonny knew that, by the sovereign grace of God, Cody's sin and his response had landed him securely in the arms of Jesus.

Cody's release from jail was still seven weeks away. Lonny knew that being back on the street would present Cody with multiple temptations. He might leave his cell with a clean heart and wholesome intentions, but he was about to enter a war zone. He would have to armor up for the fight ahead. Lonny was going to make sure Cody went into battle with one piece of equipment he didn't have before.

12

Cody Reckons Himself Dead to Sin

I N THE DAYS FOLLOWING their session on repentance, Cody spent a lot of time in his jail cell taking to heart what Lonny had said. He recommitted himself to Christ, confessing sins and asking the Holy Spirit to give him a godly mindset. He found that reading Ephesians, as Lonny had suggested, brought conviction of attitudes and behaviors he needed to confess to God.

Also, he began to notice new goals and desires form in his heart, and he asked God to fulfill them in his life.

Lonny came to their next meeting with a lot to say, so when he sat down with Cody he first made sure Cody was doing well, and then got quickly to the point. Lonny had thought of a simple illustration to teach Cody a truth he would have to live by when he is released from jail.

"Cody, let's say you are the captain of your ship and as you are sailing over the sea you realize you are going in a wrong direction, so you turn your ship around. That's repentance, what we covered last week, but that's not the total solution, because there can be storms and strong winds and cross-currents that can still push your ship off course. So I'm going to tell you of something you need to do to keep moving ahead."

Lonny took Cody to Romans 6:11, "Reckon yourselves to be dead indeed to sin, but alive to God in Christ Jesus our Lord" (NKJ). He explained that this is a command and that to *reckon* means to *count* or *consider*, so Cody must consider himself dead to sin and alive to God in Christ. A few weeks ago he had taught Cody some basics about reckoning and how it relates to faith.

Reckoning as a Way of Life

"I like to put it this way, Cody. Reckoning follows repentance and makes it a way of life. It's actually the way we maintain a constant attitude of repentance. Remember that definition of repentance I read last week. Most important, it's a change in the way we think. We begin to think biblically. Now we see the direction we were heading is just plain wrong and it won't give us the good things we used to imagine.

"Simply put, repentance is about hating our misdeeds and starting a better course of life.

"We also had fun talking about 'hearty amendments.' Those are the productive, good ways of thinking and good deeds that we do out of love. Reckoning is how we bring those hearty amendments to reality in our life. It's the way we keep that new mindset—by applying to our lives the power of the cross of Christ.

"You know a lot of what God has done for you through the cross—that when Jesus died on the cross, you died with him. When he was buried in the grave, you were buried with him. When he was raised from the dead, you were raised with him. This very chapter of Romans says all these things.

"We can know these things intellectually but they remain outside of our daily thinking and living. Reckoning applies the power of these truths to our thinking and behavior in the here and now.

Making Provision for the Right Things

"Here's a question for you that hits right to this point: after your release from this place, will you carry condoms in your billfold or backpack? If you do, you will be reckoning yourself still very much alive to that part of your old nature. Paul in another place in

Romans says not to make provision for the flesh, and that is exactly what you would be doing. Chances are you will use them at the first opportunity, because what we think or plan for in the mind usually gets carried out in action.

"We either make provision for the spirit or for the flesh. Which is it going to be?

"We either reckon ourselves to be alive to sin or dead to it. That is our choice, and we decide moment by moment. We can welcome that sin nature back into our life—resurrect it from the grave—or we can command it to stay there.

Ruthless Perseverance

"*Command* is the right word. We have to be ruthless with temptation. Remember, temptation is just wrong thinking that would take us in a wrong direction. We command it in Jesus' name to flee.

"How would you feel if the judge signs a release for you so you are now free to leave this jail, but the sheriff decides not to let you leave? I know your inner strength. You would not just cower in a corner and be 'Woe is me. Nothing ever works out for me. I guess this is the way life will always be.'"

Cody saw the point: "I'd fight that sucker all the way!"

Lonny read for Cody a passage from James, chapter 1, describing temptation as being drawn away by our own desires. "It's our desires that give birth to sin, and sin brings about death. We insist that the truth of the cross be realized in our life. No matter how strongly our own ungodly desires cry out to us, we command that they have no power over us.

"Some of this may sound strange, even impossible, Cody, but I'm telling you it works because of the power of the cross. If you stick with it, insisting that your behavior and thinking conform to Bible truth, and you persevere, you will win!"

To reinforce this point, Lonny told Cody what Jesus said about freedom: "Most assuredly, I say to you, whoever commits sin is a slave of sin. And a slave does not abide in the house forever, but a son abides forever. Therefore *if the Son makes you free, you shall be free indeed"* (John 8:34–36 NKJ). Lonny explained that this is a promise ready-made for reckoning.

"Reckon that what Jesus said is true of you. I am free indeed! Declare this truth over yourself, apply it to your life, and insist that it become true in your everyday experience. This is reckoning 101, my friend."

Freedom Is Our Birthright

Cody had a thought and wanted to know Lonny's response. "This freedom comes with being born again, right. So trying to explain it to someone, could we say it's kind of like being born in the land of the free, the USA, as opposed to some country with a dictator?"

Lonny nodded. "Clever connection, my friend. I guess we could think of freedom from sin as our birthright. But I can think of a problem with your analogy of being born in the land of the free. It seems to put us in a passive, receiving mode. Kind of like the idea that just going to church makes you a Christian. It doesn't."

Cody quickly saw the point. "True, people are born in this country and just live any way they want to. Most of my friends don't care at all about freedom or loving their country. Maybe my analogy works only if everyone is a responsible citizen. You know, take advantage of our birthright."

"So true," Lonny said. "Our freedom in Christ has been declared from heaven, so now we are responsible for pulling it down by faith and applying it to ourselves. We insist it be so, we command it be so, and we do not let up until it is the rule of our life."

Commanding the Mountain of Bitterness

Next, Lonny took aim at something he knew that Cody had to deal with, and now was the time. "Cody, I know you pretty well now. You have opened up to me, and I know a lot of the struggles you've had, the things that have been done to you starting when you were a child.

"One thing I see, if I may be so bold, is that you have some unforgiveness toward your father. I think this has been at the root of some of the things that have led you into trouble. So if you are willing, I think it would be good at this time for you to let go of that unforgiveness."

Cody agreed, and Lonny quickly thought of a way to illustrate what Cody should do. Lonny wanted Cody to see how reckoning works with a stronghold of sin such as unforgiveness.

"Picture your bitterness as a mountain," Lonny told Cody. "Remember where Jesus was teaching his disciples to have faith in God, and Jesus used the example of saying to a mountain, 'Be removed and be cast into the sea.' Jesus told them to believe that what they say will be done.

"Jesus said that in Mark 11. And right after this he went on in verses 25 and 26 to talk about forgiveness: 'And whenever you stand praying, if you have anything against anyone, forgive him, that your Father in heaven may also forgive you your trespasses. But if you do not forgive, neither will your Father in heaven forgive your trespasses.'"

Reckoning against Bitterness

Lonny explained that the first step is repentance—Cody must confess to God his resentment toward his father. But Lonny knew that Cody would still have to deal with the memories of being mistreated by his father, which would tempt Cody again to dredge up the same feelings of bitterness. Reckoning was the process Cody would have to use against the old thought patterns.

"So here's a good example of how you can reckon yourself dead to a big sin issue. Your old nature of resentment and unforgiveness died on the cross with Christ. You no longer have to yield to its power in your life. Reckon yourself dead to it!

"God has given you the authority to command that mountain of bitterness to flee. Jesus emphasized *saying* to the mountain 'Be removed and be cast into the sea.' Use your command voice. Take authority over it. Command it in Jesus' name to get out of your life."

"See how this works," Lonny pleaded. "God has given you the victory over this sin and every other stronghold in your life. So be ruthless against it. Your victory is already won so don't be passive. Take it by force."

Cody's focus and attention seemed to increase as the meeting went on. His spirit was on the move. "All that we've gone over today, what you said, I can feel more confidence, authority, resistance—all those things. The reality of strongholds. Man I've got a lot of them, and I can't wait to get back inside and start going on the attack."

The Father's Love

Seeing they had only a few minutes left, Lonny wanted to tell Cody of something God had impressed on his heart while praying for him the night before. "Cody, Jesus has had his hand on you ever since you were a child. He has seen all the things you have experienced, all the things done to you that you could not control, all the things you have done. He has been with you, knowing he would bring you through to this point in your life. Now he is repositioning you. He has turned the ship of your life to himself.

"Our heavenly Father has such love and affection for you, my friend, and I pray that he would open the eyes of your heart to see this great love that pours from his Fatherly heart to yours." With his hands on Cody's shoulders, Lonny asked Jesus to pour out the Holy Spirit on his friend, giving him a spirit of revelation of the knowledge and love of God, with a hunger for more of God's word and a sense of his abiding presence.

Cody, seeing the deputy at the door, stood, wiped his eyes, and thanked Lonny, who told him there was still another part of reckoning they would discuss next week.

13

Cody Reckons Himself Alive to God

L ONNY CAME TO THE next meeting with more to tell Cody about reckoning. They had so far been focusing on a negative: being dead to sin. Now the focus would shift to a positive: being alive to God. What Cody needed to know is that reckoning on this positive is the source of power for thriving as a Christian on planet Earth. In an ultimate sense Cody will succeed in dying to sin only through living to God.

Sitting down to the table, Cody assured Lonny he had a really good week. His expression said the same thing. He was ready to learn more.

Lonny told Cody he now wanted to explain how reckoning works in terms of being alive to God.

Hearts Beating in Tune with God

"Hey Cody, I've got a hypothetical situation for you. What I'm going to tell you is extremely bad theology, but I want you to hang with it as I make a point. It's really, really bad theology, actually. But here's the thing. Suppose God the Father, Jesus the Son, and the Holy Spirit somehow send a message to all people on Earth. They announce they are withdrawing from this universe and say they are going to create a different one. They will no longer be around. So it's basically goodbye. How would you feel?"

"Awful, man! I'd feel empty, left alone. Far worse than when my own father left us."

"Horrible thought, isn't it Cody. As for myself, I'd feel as if all the life had been sucked out of me. To lose God in our lives would be devastating. But for many others, those who don't know God, it would be nothing different. Some might celebrate—even dance in the streets, because the One who holds them accountable is gone. You see, these people are dead to God now.

"We are alive to him. Our hearts beat in tune with his. That's why we can't imagine being without him.

"Remember that there is this other side to reckoning in that verse in Romans 6. We are already alive to God in the way we were just talking about. And this verse tells us to reckon ourselves alive to God. This suggests we can become even more alive to him. So let's explore what it means to *reckon ourselves alive to God*."

Seeing Ourselves as God Sees Us

"The whole point of reckoning is to insist that what is true in the spiritual realm must become true in my experience. Remember the operational definition of reckoning we've talked about before: it's calling something that is not as though it were."

Cody seemed a bit puzzled and said, "Could you run through that again. I had this down, but now it's a bit fuzzy again."

"No problem," Lonny replied. "Let's go over this idea of *calling something that is not as though it were*. Of course, we are talking about something that really does exist, because God has said it exists. He has said our sin nature died on the cross with Christ, and we are now righteous, not because of our behavior, but because he has declared us to be righteous."

Cody said, "Okay, I'm picking up on it again. I see that what does not yet exist is our sinless behavior, but we now have the right to call ourselves righteous because of what God says about us. And he gave us a new nature."

"Right," Lonny replied. "We've already seen that God declares me dead to sin, because my sin nature died on the cross with Christ. In my spiritual position, which is in Christ, I am now dead to sin. The first step of reckoning is to see myself as God sees me. Therefore I have the right to call myself dead to sin, even though I am still from time to time struggling with sinning. It's a paradox of faith, but you see, this is how we conquer sin in practice.

"Knowing we already have victory over sin through Christ is essential for our conquering of sin in practice. So, I have the right to insist that sin no longer has control over me.

"As we do this—changing our thought process and exerting our will in accordance with what God has said is true about us—our experience will catch up with our spiritual position. We will never achieve perfection, but we'll discover sin no longer rules over us as it once did. We realize we no longer *have to* sin.

"Now, Cody, let's apply the same truth to the second part of this verse—being alive to God. God has declared that I am alive to him because he raised me from the grave in Christ. I am alive to God because of my union with Christ, and therefore I have the right to *insist* that I will be alive to him in my actual experience. This is a big-time, high-level truth and it has important implications for how we live."

Godliness Belongs to Me!

Lonny continued, "What I'm getting at is this: my feelings must give way to my will. If my experience fails to conform to God's declaration that I am alive to him, then I have the right to command that my experience fall in line. If I don't hunger and thirst after those things that build righteousness, I believe and insist and begin to act as if I do hunger and thirst for righteousness.

"I may not feel like doing some things the Bible says are godly, but I will reckon that they are mine and I will therefore insist that my experience must conform to these godly things. I will live as if I experience them now and persist in reckoning myself as experiencing them until my experience catches up with God's declaration that I am alive to him.

"It's kind of like what David says at the beginning of Psalm 103: 'Bless the LORD, O my soul; and all that is within me, bless His holy name!' David is commanding his heart to worship God."

"Wow, that's chill," Cody said. "I never would've thought of that verse as a kind of reckoning. Did David know about reckoning?"

"Good question," Lonny replied. "I don't think David would have known about it in the sense that Romans 6 talks about. But come to think of it, he was anointed king long before he actually became king, so he was reckoning himself king. He also had to have known about Abraham, who lived out reckoning. Just like Abraham, we sometimes have to wait patiently for God's declaration to come to pass. Abraham reckoned himself alive to God's promise that he would receive land as an inheritance. Well, let's see how that turned out."

Lonny turned to the following verses from Hebrews 11:

> By faith Abraham obeyed when he was called to go out to the place which he would receive as an inheritance. And he went out, not knowing where he was going. By faith he dwelt in the land of promise as *in* a foreign country, dwelling in tents with Isaac and Jacob, the heirs with him of the same promise; for he waited for the city which has foundations, whose builder and maker *is* God.

"As long as Abraham lived, the land remained only a promise. He camped on it but it never became his. But as Abraham lived on the land as a foreigner, he began to see something in his spirit that took on more importance than the ground he was walking on. He saw in his spirit the heavenly city that is built by God himself. So he lived as if he were already in the land of promise. By reckoning on what God promised, Abraham became more alive to God."

Rejoicing by Faith

Lonny explained to Cody that what he is saying is really no more than faith combined with obedience to God's will.

"Here's another example, and this is something God showed me several years ago. The Bible tells us to rejoice. Apostle Paul even says in 1 Thessalonians 5:16 to rejoice always. In the Old Testament, God told Moses to command the people to rejoice when they came together before the Lord for the feasts. They may have been cranky but they rejoiced anyway.

"Here's my point: God tells me to rejoice, so I assume that this is something that must be common to someone who is in a close relationship with God. I insist that it become common to me! Sometimes I feel cold as a catfish in my own private devotions, but I will turn on worship music and begin to worship God. Nine times out of ten the process of worshiping brings about an attitude of genuine rejoicing. The same thing happens when I come into the worship service at church.

"It's wonderful how this works, and there's nothing phony or insincere about my doing it. It's all about responding in faith to God's promise and command. And the same thing applies to reading the Bible, serving others, prayer, and anything else that brings me closer to God."

Cody was eager to say something. "I think I've been catching on to this. This morning I was reading in Psalm 119 and I found a couple verses that seem to say this very thing you are getting at. In one place is a prayer that God would open our eyes to see the truth, and another place it asks God to turn away my eyes from looking at worthless things and for God to revive me. I can see that the guy who wrote that was doing what you are saying. He was reckoning there's something good he isn't seeing very clearly but wants to, and there's a better way to see things than what he's used to—a way more alive to God. So this morning I told God I wanted the same thing those verses say."

Lonny smiled, "Man, that's really true and a good insight! Somehow the Holy Spirit lets us see a higher level of freedom and devotion to God, and then by faith we see ourselves living at that higher level and we are hungry to seek after it. Mostly we become hungrier for God himself. Just like in your case, this happens often when we are reading the Bible.

"What you said hits on all the ingredients of reckoning ourselves alive to God. It includes God's truth, his awakening of our hope and curiosity by his promises, our faith in his goodness, and especially our desire for more of him, plus our obedience," Lonny concluded, his voice rising with every phrase.

"Seems like God put things in the word to entice us," Cody said, "like he wants us to be curious and seek after more of him. Before my dad got weird, I remember him one time playing hide and seek with us kids. He'd hide from us so we would try to find him. In God's case, he wants us to desire him and he puts clues in his word telling how to get closer to him."

Cody stood up. "What you say really does go deep. I'll read those chapters and think this over, but now I've got to go. The guard's name is Bernard and I'm on his good side. He even gave us extra time together, but I don't want to take it for granted.

"I always look forward to this time with you, and I so much appreciate your help and prayers. I feel like my life is on an upward slope, and for the first time I really do know God is for me, that I can trust him to do good to me. Amazing, isn't it, that I can say this while still in jail! Say hello to the guys at church."

"I'll see you next week," Lonny said, "and good as this has been I think we're still not quite done with reckoning ourselves alive to God."

14

Lonny Explains Sexual Purity in the New Covenant

THIS WEEK LONNY DECIDED to bring up sexual sin Cody will need to avoid when he leaves prison. He thought the best way to address this issue would be to show Cody from Scripture why sexual purity is important to God. The more alive to God Cody becomes, the stronger will be his motivation to do things God's way.

The meeting began with Cody's need for some advice about a conflict he was having with another prisoner. Once Cody was satisfied he knew how to handle that situation, Lonny moved on. "Cody, I know only a little about your past in regard to sexual experiences, but I'm certain you will have to deal with these temptations after you leave this place. So is it okay to talk about this?"

Cody nodded. "I know this could be a problem just like it's been in the past, and I've already been praying about it, also confessing past stuff. So yeah, let's talk."

Lonny wanted to take sex beyond the typical list of do's and don'ts and reframe the subject so Cody could look at it more from God's perspective.

"We had a young guy in our church years ago who didn't like being told sex before marriage was wrong. He was having sex with girlfriends, one after another, and didn't want to stop. He read through the Old Testament and came up with what he thought of as permission or at least lack of restrictions, so he told our leadership we were being legalistic beyond what the Bible says. Eventually he left the church, and now does not profess Christ."

"So was he right about the Old Testament?" Cody asked.

"The message there is a bit complicated, Cody," Lonny replied. "Abraham, Jacob, David all had multiple wives or concubines and were not condemned for it. It was even permissible, though not to the extent of moral approval, for a man to go to a prostitute. Judah has sex with Tamar, thinking she is a prostitute, but the way the Bible presents it, his misdeed wasn't that he had sex with a prostitute but rather that he had dishonored Tamar by not giving his youngest son to marry her. You can read about this in Genesis 38.

"Proverbs 2 does warn against sex outside of marriage," Lonny explained, and he also showed Cody several passages from Leviticus and the prophetic books that highlight God's clear intent for his people's sexual purity.

The Mystery of One Flesh

Cody was eager to hear more, but said he was still puzzled by what appears to be a mixed message in the Old Testament. Lonny told him to listen closely to what he was about to share. The New Testament commands are quite clear, but Lonny wanted Cody to understand not only the commands but also the biblical rationale for them.

Typical teaching on sex, he told Cody, presents the commands along with some pragmatic reasons to abstain, such as avoiding STDs. "Pragmatics don't cut it with most young people, because they figure they can avoid any consequences, and they are probably right. Sex is more important than any practical consequences anyway, they might think. The difficulty with trying to explain the reason those commands are in the Bible is that it takes effort to understand the Bible, and frankly we encounter a bit of a mystery when we come to the New Testament. Even many mature Christians don't understand it so they don't try to explain it to young people. So no wonder kids acted out sexually."

Lonny said that to make the teaching of the New Testament understandable he would take Cody back to God's original command in regard to sex.

"The ideal, of course, is what God laid out for Adam and Eve in Genesis 2:24. God said, 'a man shall leave his father and mother and be joined to his wife, and they shall become one flesh.' So keep this verse in mind as we get to the New Testament, where sexual sin is a lot more clearly defined.

"Paul says in Ephesians 5 that people who are sexually immoral or impure have no inheritance in the kingdom of Christ. And he says the same thing in 1 Corinthians 6. Let's go there because that's where this topic takes an important turn we need to understand. I think we find there why sex is regarded in the New Testament in a way quite different from the Old.

"Here in 1 Corinthians 6 Paul brings up the marriage passage in Genesis 2, and he makes what seems to be a strange point. He says that to have sex with a prostitute is to be one body with her, which is similar to the husband and wife becoming one flesh."

"But that's still Old Testament," Cody interjected. "So what's strange about that?"

Lonny continued. "What is strange is how he then makes the point in verse 17 that the believer is joined to the Lord and is one spirit with the Lord. 'Strange' maybe isn't the right word, but what he is saying is remarkable. It jumps right out at us. He's talking about our union with Christ. In verse 15 he says our bodies are members of Christ, so to join our bodies to a harlot is to join Christ with a harlot. The same is true of having sex with anyone outside of marriage.

"There is a lot more in this passage, but now let's go to Ephesians 5 where the point I want you to see becomes clearer. Here is where we do encounter something of a mystery, though. But I think you'll be excited to learn this.

The Mystical Union with Christ

"You can see already in 1 Corinthians 6 that Paul regards sexual behavior as more than a physical act. It's a spiritual union. For the Christian, sex has a deeply spiritual meaning because of our union with Christ. In verse 30 of Ephesians 5 Paul again makes the point that we are members of Christ's body.

"Then in the next verse he quotes the Genesis 2 'one flesh' passage just as he did in Corinthians. And in the verse after that, verse 32, he says, 'This is a profound mystery—but I am talking about Christ and the church.' This profound mystery Paul talks about has to do with what theologians call the mystical union between Christ and his body the church.

"So this is why, Cody, sexual sin in the New Testament comes under such condemnation. A few verses before this we see that Christ loved the church and gave up his life for her to make her holy. Marriage between a loving husband and a submitted wife in a mysterious way models the intimate union of Christ and his bride."

Cody said, "I get it now. So that's why Paul says having sex outside of marriage is to join Christ with a prostitute. I am joined with Christ, so if I join myself to a prostitute I also join Christ to that prostitute. Something spiritual happens. When you had the Bible open to that Corinthians chapter, I saw there that our bodies are the temple of the Holy Spirit and we no longer even own our bodies. So if Christ bought our bodies, I guess the price was his death on the cross—right?"

"Totally right, it was his shed blood," Lonny emphasized. "Now we belong to Christ, and our bodies are for the Lord. Paul says the Lord is also for *our* bodies, which means there is a blessing on our bodies when we yield them to him."

Reckoning Ourselves Christ's Holy Bride

Lonny remembered an important verse in 2 Corinthians 11 that he wanted to share with Cody. Paul the apostle said he wanted to present the Corinthian believers to Christ as a pure virgin. Paul's motivation behind that desire was a subject Lonny decided he would save for a later meeting with Cody. For now, he wanted Cody to see how important it is to God that we grow in sanctification to become a holy and pure bride for our future marriage to Christ.

So Lonny read and explained verse 2: "For I feel a divine jealousy for you, since I betrothed you to one husband, to present you as a pure virgin to Christ."

"Right now we are in the engagement stage in this love relationship with Christ," he said. "We have been betrothed to him as a pure virgin. That's what Paul says in this verse. Then when Christ returns, we will be presented to him as his holy and pure bride. If we who are now betrothed to him engage in sex outside of marriage we violate that sacred betrothal."

"Think of it this way, Cody. Our identity as believers is *in Christ*. We reckon this to be true, and we reckon ourselves dead to all sin, including sexual. On the positive side, we also reckon ourselves alive to God, because he raised us from the grave in Christ so that we would live for him. This includes using our bodies for the purpose he designed.

"Christ already thinks of us as his holy bride so we are to reckon ourselves accordingly, and now we live to satisfy his desire that his bride be holy and blameless. So we submit ourselves to his purpose and will."

Voluntary Celibacy

Lonny thought of a way to finish this talk about sex that would drive home a couple additional points. First, he wanted Cody to understand the voluntary nature of our commitment to Christ. Second, he wanted to set the stage for an important subject he would bring up next week.

"Cody, did you know Daniel was a eunuch? I'm talking about Daniel the Old Testament prophet. You know about Daniel in the lion's den and how his friends escaped the fiery furnace, plus all the dreams he interpreted."

"Of course," Cody replied, "but you mean his stuff was cut off? He was such a powerful guy it's hard to believe."

Lonny told him of a passage in Isaiah that makes it clear Daniel and his Jewish friends were emasculated as teenagers when they were selected to serve in Nebuchadnezzar's court. "The king wanted them to have no other desire but to serve him. He knew their sexuality would be a distraction, so he cut it off.

"Think about that, Cody. Unlike Nebuchadnezzar, our King lets us keep our balls! Jesus is not afraid of our sexuality. Obviously he created our sexuality. He knows our sexual desire may get in the way of serving him. But he also knows we will grow so devoted to him, so attracted to his beauty and willing to yield to his Lordship, that at some point we will make a decision to voluntarily put our sexuality at the foot of the cross. We will volunteer to be his holy and chaste bride.

"This doesn't mean we give up sex, Cody. We don't make ourselves eunuchs. Instead we choose to use sex for the purpose he created."

"You see how God is glorified not by forcing us to serve him but by our choice to serve him. Nebuchadnezzar has been forgotten, but all over the world people are still serving the King of Kings. Our choice to serve and obey him demonstrates to everyone that he is worthy of our devotion and sacrifice, and no worldly or physical pleasure can match the pleasure we find in him—now and forever. He doesn't force that recognition on us. He *invites* our devotion. He seeks voluntary lovers.

"Next week we'll talk about desiring what he desires. I can't wait."

Cody stood up with a big smile. "I can't wait either. Now I think I'll go reread the book of Daniel."

15

Cody Aligns His Desire
With God's Desire

Lonny greeted Cody, "Hey jailbird, how you doing?" Cody laughed back, "Never felt freer!"

Cody went on, "All this reckoning you've been laying on me has really got me thinking. It's spiritually inspiring, for sure. But I'm also seeing life differently. I was working out with the weights they've got here, and I was visualizing myself bigger and flatter— you know. I had a picture in my mind of what I want my body to look like, and while working out I realized I'm *reckoning* that I will look like that image in my mind if I just keep working on it."

Cody was clearly excited as he continued. "I can see what you mean now. We must insist that what God says about us must become true in our experience. In these spiritual things, I'm getting an image of who God says I am, and that gives me the motivation to believe it and work toward it. Thinking that way really does motivate me!"

"What a great analogy, Cody! Reckoning yourself ripped—I love it! You visualized it, believed it, counted it yours, and lifted the weights. You became alive to your fit future self." Lonny could hardly contain his own excitement at seeing Cody grab ahold of these life-giving biblical truths they have been discussing for the past several weeks.

He did point out to Cody that although he was thinking of reckoning in the same way the Bible does, there is a difference between reckoning on the basis of a goal Cody set for himself and reckoning on the basis of what God has already done for us.

But the analogy is excellent, he told Cody, for showing the connection between reckoning and effort. Just as you can't add muscle just by picturing yourself ripped, reckoning oneself dead to sin has to be combined with active effort. We have to enforce the word of God in our thoughts and behavior.

A Foundational Question

Cody had rededicated his life to Christ and his mental outlook was being transformed week by week, but Lonny knew that Cody would face many challenges following his release from jail, including sexual temptations as they had discussed last week. It was time to introduce Cody to another biblical truth, one that is more foundational than reckoning but becomes real in our life through reckoning.

Lonny had seen all too often what happens when young people set out to live for Christ without knowing the crucial reason, the biblical reason why the people of the Lord lay down their lives for him. Once they make this discovery, they no longer need to be told why they *should* surrender their lives to Christ. They voluntarily and gladly *do* surrender.

People of the Lord gladly yield to him when they discover something about God that is far more attractive than any of the pleasures and delights of this world.

Lonny remembered a question Cody had a couple weeks ago. He wanted to know why God wants us to do things his way. That's a pretty good question for today's meeting, Lonny thought. What *is* God's way? Lonny didn't want to wade far into the deep water of the divine purpose, but he did want Cody to know something about what God wants from us, because knowing what God desires has a way of transforming our desires and leading us to a deeper surrender to the divine will.

God seeks the devotion of our heart, and now Lonny wanted to expand Cody's vision of God so as to awaken the core of his desire for those things God desires. The Christian life comes down to the object of our desire—why we conform our will to God's will, our desire to his desire, our passion to his passion. Lonny wanted this day to help Cody acquire a new passion.

Lonny reminded Cody of his question about having to do things God's way and said he would like to answer it as best he could.

What Does God Desire?

"Let's look again at reckoning for the answer to that question you had about why God wants us to do things his way. A big part of being *alive* to someone is to truly know them—to understand what they like and dislike—because then we know how to please them. Reckoning ourselves alive to God starts with knowing what pleases God.

"Paul tells us in the first chapter of Ephesians what pleases God. The Father seeks to sum everything up in Jesus Christ. The Father's passion centers on his Son! That's also clear from the booming voice the Father spoke from heaven when Jesus was baptized and when he was transfigured. Remember the Transfiguration when John and Peter saw Jesus in his radiant glory and they heard the Father say, 'Behold my beloved Son in whom I am well pleased!'

"We also know, as we saw last week, that the Father is preparing us to be a suitable bride for his Son. So the Father is sanctifying and cleansing us, removing every spot or wrinkle, to make us a holy and pure bride. This is also the passion of Jesus himself. Paul even says in Ephesians 5 that Jesus will present us to himself. So Jesus is preparing his own bride!

"We read where Paul says that husbands are to love their wives just as Christ loved the church and gave himself for the church. He died for his bride and now he is sanctifying his bride.

"Our holiness is what both the Father and the Son long for. Doesn't it make perfect sense, then, that if we reckon ourselves alive to the Father and the Son, we will want to cooperate with the process they have chosen to make us a suitable bride? We should want to be holy because that is what they desire for us. This is how we conform our passion to their passion.

"Cody, this is where the motivation comes from to live righteously. This is the most powerful motivation I know. Nothing else compares. It's far greater than satisfying any worldly desire we might have—even a desire for a good and godly thing.

"We can say that if we live righteously we will enjoy our lives more. That's probably true, and the book of Proverbs draws attention to the rewards of righteous living, but if we make the seeking of enjoyment our primary goal, it may not keep us pointed in the right direction over the long term. Self-interest always fails in the end unless we become convinced our greatest joy, our greatest rewards, come from serving God's interest. Only in that sense should our self-interest be our motive."

"Is there anything in it for us?" Cody wanted to know. He quickly added, "I know that sounds selfish and it's similar to my wanting to know why we have to do things God's way. But I'm trying to get my mind around the idea of total surrender to God. You know, that's a tough concept."

Reciprocal Love in the Godhead

"Maybe this will help, Cody." Lonny thought of the concept of reciprocal love and hoped it would expand Cody's perspective. "You understand now that reckoning ourselves alive to God puts us in the mindset of wanting to love and please God. So what I want to do now is give you a little wider perspective of why we should want to love and please God.

"The Godhead is a community of three persons—Father, Son, and Holy Spirit. The Bible tells us that God is love. Love is his nature, his essence, and the three persons of the Trinity express their love for one another through mutual self-surrender, which is another way of expressing sacrificial love. This reciprocal love is at the center of the Godhead and of the image of God.

"Cody, you could spend a lifetime meditating on this truth and I encourage you to do that because it will rivet your heart on the beauty of the heart of God. Down the road a ways I hope we will have the time to talk much more about this, and we can look through the Bible for the many places it shows up. I am telling you also that once we understand this quality of God it clarifies so much about our relationship with God and with one another.

"When you get a chance, read chapters 14 through 17 of the Gospel of John. You will see clearly there the mutual love between the Father and Son. They bring glory to each other and give everything they have to each other. The Spirit participates in the same way, bringing glory to the Son, testifying about the Son, and giving access to the Father."

The Divine Drama

Cody then said something that showed he was clearly catching on to the implications of what Lonny was telling him. "Seems like there has to be a connection between this reciprocating love between the Father, Son, and Holy Spirit and why they want us to love them. This really opens things up for me. It's as if they want us to join their community of love."

"There you go, Cody, you just nailed it! The nature of their love is that they want to reach outward beyond themselves and love others. The Father is adding adopted children to the divine family who will seek the interests of their fellow members and regard others as more important than themselves. Quite a glorious drama we get to play a role in, isn't it!

"The Father adopted us as his children, and this gives us a good way to think of sanctification. It's his process of training us to live as responsible members of his family. Hebrews 12 talks about God's discipline of us so we are not illegitimate children but learn to share his holiness. As responsible children, we learn to obey and honor our Father and conform our will to his. This is how we love him.

"And it doesn't end with us loving them. Now you know why we find all those verses about loving and serving one another in the community of God's people, the church. I think in John 15 alone Jesus gives at least two commands to love one another. And that's where he says, 'Greater love has no one than this, that he lay down his life for his friends.'

"So once we understand God's heart, we know why he gives us the commandments he does. And we see more clearly how to please him. The Father delights to see us love him and love one another with purity of heart. He also knows we will be happiest when we do things his way. His way is the best way for him and for us."

Satisfying God's Passion for a Holy People

"Oh, one more thing. I almost forgot to show you this before our time is up—I want you to see how this desire to satisfy God's desire motivated the Apostle Paul. Remember that verse in 2 Corinthians, chapter 11, I told you about last week. Paul told the Corinthian church he was jealous for them because of his desire to present them as a chaste virgin to Christ. See what he's saying. Paul caught the vision.

"Paul knows God's passion for his people to become that holy and pure bride, so Paul has aligned his passion with God's. He knows the Father and the Son are preparing their bride, so Paul's motivation in serving the church is to satisfy Christ's passion for a holy bride. Paul is serving the bridegroom to bring him his heart's desire—a holy church as his bride.

"Cody, I've caught that same passion! And that's why I delight in coming here to meet with you. I want to present you to Christ as a holy and pure bride! I fully believe you too will catch this same vision and go on from here to train and equip others."

Cody saw the guard and realized their time was up. "Okay, old man, you've given me a lot more to think about. This is solid stuff. Good answer to my question, and I can see how reckoning myself alive to God brings me right to what you're saying about his desire and making it my desire."

Three days later Cody got an early release from jail. That night he walked into the church's fellowship room in time for Lonny's weekly Bible study—on Romans.

. . .

In the months and years following his incarceration, Cody continued on the upward trajectory of his walk with Christ. He continued to meet frequently with his mentor Lonny, who introduced Cody to the chaplain of a youth correctional facility. Soon Cody was playing basketball and counseling with the teenage inmates. Four years after his release, Cody married the lead singer of the church's worship group. He and his wife have two children and lead a life group in their home. He manages a security firm started by two of Lonny's business associates. Cody's favorite saying is, "Mercy triumphs over judgment."

PART 5

Lifelong Love and Surrender

CODY, WITH LONNY'S TUTELAGE, escaped the bondages of stealing, promiscuity, and bitterness by applying the principle of reckoning. Once he understood that God's gift of righteousness by faith and his union with Christ in death, burial, and resurrection set him free from the domination of sin, he set his will to yield no longer to those things that had kept him captive.

Cody also learned to reckon himself alive to God, and the Holy Spirit opened his heart to the things of God in Scripture. He laid a foundation of faith and knowledge for living in close fellowship with God the remainder of his life. We can be confident that God will complete the good work he began in Cody (Phil 1:7).

One ministry of the Spirit is to bind our heart to God so that we persevere in lifelong devotion to him. He is the "Spirit of adoption by whom we cry out, 'Abba, Father,'" and he confirms to us throughout life's inevitable and unavoidable trials that we are the Father's beloved children (Rom 8:15–16).

I explain in chapter 16 how the Holy Spirit used a passage in Hebrews to bind my heart to God. Chapter 17 is my testimony of surrender to the hand of God, and, finally, I tell in chapter 18 how God surprised me with his love.

"*Therefore, since we have so great a cloud of witnesses surrounding us, let us also lay aside every encumbrance and the sin which so easily entangles us, and let us run with endurance the race that is set before us, fixing our eyes on Jesus, the author and perfecter of faith.*" *(Heb 12:1–2 NASB)*

16

The Divine Attraction

WHAT DO YOU FIND most attractive about God? You can probably compile a long mental list of things that attract you to God. He's your Savior and Provider. He disarmed your enemy, the devil. He comforts you in your afflictions. He is love, and the fountain of mercy and truth. As sovereign, eternal, omniscient, and omnipotent Lord, he reigns over all creation. What could be more attractive about God?

When I ask believers what qualities they find most attractive about God, many are quick to say his faithfulness. Others point to his love, majesty, holiness, kindness, mercy, or patience. Most mention the sense of peace they experience when in his presence. One thing we can all agree on is that there are a lot of things about God worthy of our adoration.

Nearly every page of Scripture offers sufficient reason to worship God forever. Among all these attractions found in God, one especially endears him to me. It's a quality of his character that tugs at my heart as nothing else does. I turn to it again and again for inspiration in my quiet times and for strength in trials.

The attributes of God are like facets on a diamond, each revealing one aspect of the divine beauty. In the center of the diamond is the divine heart. For God, as for humans, the heart is the center or core of being. God's heart is distinct from his attributes yet is inseparable from them. From this center, the glorious light and love of God radiate through the facets of the diamond, inviting us to discover the source of this beauty in the heart of God.

The Offense of the Cross

The best window I've found for peering into the divine heart is a short phrase of only six words in the second chapter of Hebrews. I run to this passage whenever I need a fresh reminder of why God the Father and Jesus the Son are worthy of my devotion. This phrase has been for me what dwelling in the house of the Lord was for David and camping out in the tent was to Joshua—a holy place to enjoy the goodness of God and usher me into his presence.

We'll get to the passage soon, but its meaning is clearer with some background.

The book of Hebrews was written to a community of Jewish converts to Christianity. Because persecution in the Roman world at that time targeted Christians more than Jews, these converts were tempted to abandon their belief in Jesus the Messiah and find relative safety in their original Judaism. The author warns them that doing so would incur God's judgment. "Take care, brethren, that there not be in any one of you an evil, unbelieving heart that falls away from the living God" (Heb 3:12).

Much of Hebrews, especially the first two chapters, is an argument for the superiority of Christ. He is creator and heir of all that is; he is the radiance of God's glory and exact likeness of God's nature; he now sits at the Father's right hand; angels worship him. But there is one issue the author must have a good answer for: Jews did not like the concept of their Messiah hung on a tree, and surely we can sympathize with them.

Who isn't repulsed by crucifixion? Even uttering the word in public was offensive to the Romans. But to the Jews, who expected their Messiah to come in regal glory and restore the preeminence the nation enjoyed under David, the cross of Christ was all the more repugnant. It was, as Paul says, their stumbling block.

Already desiring to escape persecution, these believers' wariness of the cross was another reason to second-guess their decision to follow Christ. Why should they continue to put faith in a suspect cause that seems only to bring more suffering on them?

The author knows that certain Jewish teachers were using this very argument to persuade his readers to abandon Christianity.

So in verse 9 of chapter 2, when the author first mentions the Messiah's "suffering of death," he has a choice to make. How is he going to defend the cross? Should he plod through a lengthy theological justification? No, he decides. He instead pens a single sentence that is one of the most remarkable verses in all of Scripture. It is both majestic in eloquence and packed with revelation.

As you slowly read verse 10, ponder the breadth of its subject matter: God's sovereign claim over all that he has made, the destiny he has planned for his children, the mission and work of Jesus Christ, and the role of suffering in our salvation. And this list doesn't even include the truth we will shortly discover in the opening phrase.

> For it was fitting for Him, for whom are all things, and through whom are all things, in bringing many sons to glory, to perfect the author of their salvation through sufferings. (Heb 2:10 NASB)

Why Jesus Had to Die

Our attention now fixes on those first six words. In answer to the question in his readers' minds about why the Messiah had to die, here's what the author of Hebrews says: the suffering of Jesus as the means of our salvation needs no further justification than *it fits who God is*. At first glance, this statement seems unremarkable. We make a mistake, however, if we casually read on without pondering the profound truth conveyed by this simple phrase. A treasure of sublime beauty beckons us to stop, unravel its meaning, and gaze.

We who've been redeemed by our Savior's act of self-sacrifice readily see the logic of the substitutionary atonement. We know the cross was necessary to cleanse fallen humanity of sin without violating God's justice. The author of Hebrews will eventually get to these and other details about the work of our great High Priest.

But for now, he directs our attention to where this plan for our salvation originated: in the very heart of God. He says, in effect, "Here's something you should know up front: God willingly chose to suffer and die for you because it's in his nature to do so."

Submission to the cross, with all its agony and shame, came naturally to him. It accorded with his nature. No other reason need be given for Jesus' death. This simple yet elegant statement closes the argument.

If you want to know who God truly is in the core of his being, look at the cross. It is where he lays his heart bare for all to see. This center of the diamond is glorious indeed, and the archaic language of King James brings its supreme beauty into even sharper focus. KJ renders this phrase "It became Him." Even today, when a woman tries on a new dress, we might hear one of her friends say, "It becomes you." Her friend is noting that the dress is attractive on her. It fits who she is. It brings out her true beauty.

Look at the bloodstained cross. Repulsive? Yes. Offensive? Yes. Now look closer, into the heart of him who bled and died there for you. Can you see with eyes of faith how the cross truly "becomes" God, because it brings out his resplendent beauty? Nothing could be more attractive.

A Supreme Beauty Ignored

The cross stumbles many people even today. You've probably heard more than one person say, "I cannot respect a God who would kill his own son." I remember a twenty-year-old Japanese student who came to our church. He had heard about the shedding of animal blood in the Old Testament, and he told me he did not think the animals should have had to die. He also did not think Jesus should have died for him. Such violence was distasteful to him.

We try to manufacture a God we can live comfortably with, who conforms to our own image of how God should behave. A minister of a Unity church wrote a column in our local paper in which she applauded the statement, "The God you believe in is your vote for the kind of world you want to live in." She was pleased to think that her enlightened idea of God could create her own experience.

This attitude seems to be getting more popular. A few years ago, *The New York Times Magazine* polled a cross-section of people about their basic beliefs. "Americans increasingly decide which God best suits their temperament," the magazine concluded. We "want a capacious God who smiles on everyone, not a jealous God protective of one particular version of his teachings."[1]

If people would think for a moment about who this God really is (the eternal, sovereign, self-sufficient Creator of the universe), perhaps they would cease trying to remake him in their own image and instead humble themselves before him. Perhaps they would concede it's his prerogative to come in a form of his choosing, not theirs.

That's one of the messages of Hebrews 2:10. We place ourselves in judgment of God when we question his actions. Only God has the right to say what is fitting for him to do.

Sacrifices Admired

At this point in his argument, the author of Hebrews decided not to get into a prolonged logical explanation why the cross was necessary. But in reality, he made a simple statement that is deeply and profoundly theological: at the heart of God is perfect sacrificial love. Others, too, testify to this truth.

- Greater love has no one than this, than to lay down one's life for his friends. (John 15:13 NKJ)

- The Son of Man did not come to be served, but to serve, and to give His life a ransom for many. (Jesus, in Matt 20:28 NKJ)

---

1. Wolfe, "The Pursuit of Autonomy."

- This is how we know what love is: Jesus Christ laid down his life for us. And we ought to lay down our lives for our brothers and sisters. (1 John 3:16 NIV)

- Very rarely will anyone die for a righteous man, though for a good man someone might possibly dare to die. But God demonstrates his own love for us in this: While we were still sinners, Christ died for us. (Rom 5:7–8 NIV)

Nothing is more worthy than God's heart of sacrificial love; nothing calls more unresistingly to our own hearts. And this is why those who toss aside the God who is for a god they manufacture to fit their own preferences are so utterly foolish.

I've noticed a remarkable inconsistency in people's attitudes. Although it's fashionable to ignore or disdain God's act of self-sacrifice, everyone admires the same character quality when they see it in other people.

On the day terrorists flew airliners into the World Trade Center, the firefighters who rushed to the scene exemplified this greater love. A couple months after 9/11, Peggy Noonan wrote a column about Father George Rutler, a Roman Catholic priest who ran to the towers after the attack.

> [As the firemen] passed the priest on the way to the buildings they'd pause for a moment and ask for prayers, for a blessing, for the sacrament of confession. Soon they were lined up to talk to him in rows, "like troops before battle," he told me. He took quick confessions, and finally gave general absolution "the way you do in a war, for this was a war."
>
> When I heard this story it stopped me dead in my tracks because it told me what I'd wondered. They knew. The firemen knew exactly what they were running into, knew the odds, and yet they stood in line, received the sacrament, hoisted the hoses on their backs and charged.
>
> When Father Rutler hears sirens now his eyes fill with tears. There was so much goodness in that terrible place! And he saw it, saw the huge towers burning, melting, saw a thousand Americans hit the scene and lead what is now known, in New York, as the greatest and

most successful rescue effort on American soil in all of American history.[2]

Why is it that the act of fire fighters, police officers, lifeguards, and brave bystanders risking their own lives to save others touches something deep in our souls? I believe it is because we bear the image of the One whose willingness to sacrifice himself is at the core of his nature. God planted in our souls this admiration of sacrifice as a part of what it means to be the image of God, and even those who reject God bear a vestige of that image.

Sacrifice for the good of another is universally regarded as the supreme moral act precisely because it is the centerpiece of the moral beauty of God. Noonan wrote, "There was so much goodness in that terrible place!" This is especially true of the cross. It's where the greatest love and the deepest sorrow meet, where amidst the pain and the shame eyes of faith glimpse a goodness and a beauty.

2. Noonan, "What We Have Learned."

17

Surrender to His Ways

WHEN WE DISCOVER THE God who is—who at great cost suffered for us—we find him to be lovely, holy, beautiful, worthy, and good. We also discover that God has a purpose for us and that he is ruthless in accomplishing his purpose. Throughout the history of Christianity others have experienced these two sides of God:

> In all your journey as a believer, you will have two categories of spiritual experiences. One is tender, delightful, and loving. The other can be quite obscure, dry, dark, and desolate. God gives us the first one to gain us; he gives us the second to purify us.
>
> —Michael Molinos, a 17th-century spirituality writer[1]

In the previous chapter I described my discovery of God's beauty. I told how I came upon an obscure phrase in Hebrews 2:10 that turned a Bible study into a lifetime romance. As Michael Molinos might have said, God gained my devotion. It's the difference between knowing about God and falling in love with him.

This chapter describes the other side of my spiritual experience—God's purifying work. God knows that we must experience his enrapturing to endure his shaping, which frankly hurts. My experience also bears witness to the truth that God's compassion

---

1. Molinos, "Two Spiritual Experiences," 79.

increases in proportion to our suffering, as Paul assures us in 2 Corinthians 1.

I was diagnosed with spinal muscular atrophy (SMA) at the beginning of my senior year in high school. From the time my muscles began to weaken in my early teens I struggled with bitterness and fear of an uncertain future. I trusted in Christ at age twenty-four but my anguish continued into my late twenties.

Here is the question I had to answer: was I willing to yield to God's idea of who I should become? Just as one verse, Hebrews 2:10, attracted me to God's heart of sacrificial love, another verse, John 15:2, led my surrender to the Father's discipline. I was surprised to learn that God was already at work in my life and that he was using ways I was not recognizing as his ways. I was even resisting those ways, thinking they could not possibly be of his doing.

The Vinedresser's Pruning

One day while reading the Gospel of John I came upon Jesus' statement about the Vinedresser: "Every branch in me that does not bear fruit, he takes away; and every branch that bears fruit, he prunes it, that it may bear more fruit" (John 15:2 NASB). In previous readings of this passage, I had reasoned I could accept some pruning if it made me a more productive fruit-bearer. Isn't this how we console ourselves? We can endure some pain if we're convinced we'll come out better in the end. This time, taking the perspective of the one who does the pruning, I saw things differently.

Shortly after Christine and I were married, we landscaped our backyard with the help of my dad, who was an expert in such things. We selected rhododendrons for the color and timing of their bloom and placed the plants to show off their features. After each growing season we snipped off branches that were in the wrong place. Once again contemplating that verse in John 15, I saw the comparison. Who determined what those plants should look like? We did. We wanted to shape them for our enjoyment when they bloomed.

Who determines what I am to look like? The Vinedresser. God the Father snips away at wrong attitudes, sin patterns, narrow vision, and unsightly behaviors, guided by his own idea of the character I should have and the fruit I should bear. "By this my Father is glorified, that you bear much fruit and so prove to be my disciples" (John 15:8).

Pruning with a Mean Streak

I learned a lot about gardening from a radio talk show featuring Duane Hatch, a retired extension agent. One day a man called with a question about pruning some young fruit trees. He was shocked when Duane told him to cut out the main center branch so each tree would spread out for an easier harvest. "These are just young trees and they look so good now," the caller said.

Responding to the man's fear that pruning would hurt his trees, Duane said, "To grow a plant, you have to have a little mean streak in you."

Duane's point is this: you are the gardener. You have a purpose in mind for the plant. You want it to produce fruit, and you want to pick the fruit without risking your life on a ladder. So whack the tree now before it grows too tall to control it. Be ruthless in shaping the tree to fit your goals. And the tree itself, if you follow Duane's recommendations, will be healthier in the long run.

Does our Vinedresser have a mean streak? From our perspective, when he's cutting away at our pride and reshaping attitudes, it certainly feels that way. But as the gardener he knows we will bear more fruit.

Training for Righteousness

The key passage on the Father's discipline of his children is in Hebrews 12. "It is for discipline that you have to endure. God is treating you as sons. For what son is there whom his father does not discipline?" (verse 7). The discipline may seem painful, "but later it yields the peaceful fruit of righteousness to those who have been trained by it" (verse 11).

The Father *scourges* every son he receives (verse 6), and we find the same Greek word in Luke 18:32 where it is translated *flog*. Yes, it is where Jesus tells his disciples the Son of Man will be handed over to the Gentiles, who will mock, insult, spit on, flog and kill him. As Jesus was flogged, so are we. Although our loving Father has a much different motive than the spiteful Roman soldiers, he is sternly serious that no child of his will escape rigorous training.

Who among us would have come up with the idea of being conformed to the image of Christ, let alone would have chosen the process? I didn't raise my hand toward heaven and volunteer, "Father, I want to be like Jesus, and I don't care how much it hurts." Because God chooses the goal, he has the right to choose the means. Our job is to surrender both to the goal and to the process. Preoccupation with my own goals caused me to resent spinal muscular atrophy for messing up my life. At my worst times, I complained bitterly to God over loss of physical strength. Even as I continued to seek physical healing, and still do, what God knew I needed as well was the healing of my soul.

As I began to see things through the lens of the Vinedresser's purpose, I learned to trust that the Father was molding me into the kind of person he desired, a fit son, more like Jesus. God wanted me free from bitterness and other bondages so that I could contend for others' freedom. One Christian leader has said, "Christian maturity does not come with the passage of time, but by the right responses to the dealings of God."

Making His Desire My Desire

DeVern Fromke, in *The Ultimate Intention*, calls on believers to change our perspective: focus less on what *we* gain from salvation and seek to satisfy the Father's intention to carve out a family of sons who share the character of Jesus. Fromke's challenge to live for the pleasure and honor of the Father struck a chord in me. As

I yielded more to the Father's desire, I discovered the pleasure of pleasing him (Eph 1:5).

The Father will not relent from his work of conforming us to the image of his Son. He didn't change his Son's circumstances— even when Jesus pleaded that the cup of sorrow pass him by. He may or may not change our circumstances, but he will use them to make sure we, like Jesus, learn obedience through our sufferings (Heb 2:10, 5:8).

How Much Suffering Is Enough?

We can answer this question by employing a bit of logic. Consider these four premises and see if you agree with my conclusion:

- God has a purpose for me. (Eph 1:3–12; Rom 8:28–29)

- God uses suffering as one of the means to achieve his purpose. (Rom 8:16–17; 1 Pet 4:1–2; Phil 1:29; Heb 12:6)

- God is all-powerful. (Jude 24–25)

- God is good. (Ps 34:8)

- *Conclusion: God will use the least amount of suffering in my life necessary to achieve his purpose.*

We will experience much less pain and far greater joy if we surrender to God sooner rather than later. God constrained me at times with discipline to close off options that he knew would lead to more pain, so I thank him for the guardrails he wisely and tenderly set around me.

It Matters What We Look at

One other Bible passage offers a godly perspective on suffering.

> For momentary, light affliction is producing for us an eternal weight of glory far beyond all comparison, while we look not at the things which are seen, but at the things which are not seen; for the things which are seen are

temporal, but the things which are not seen are eternal. (2 Cor 4:17–18 NASB)

Paul says affliction produces glory. The affliction is confined to our lifetime on earth, whereas we will enjoy the glory forever. However bad the earthly affliction is, and I hope yours is brief and light, it is inconsequential in comparison with the future glory. If affliction were a stock, it would be a bargain. The more shares we buy now, the greater our windfall of glory!

But there's a catch. Paul says *while* we look. Other translations say *provided* or *since* or *as long as,* correctly rendering what is in the Greek a condition. The production of glory is not automatic but depends on setting the eyes of our heart on those unseen things.

Focusing on our painful circumstances, we may doubt God's goodness and think he does not care. With that attitude, our suffering will produce no spiritual benefit now or in eternity, because affliction has no value in itself. The ingredient that converts affliction to glory is faith—trust in the goodness of God and in his sovereign power to transform the ugly and painful things in our lives into eternal beauty. Faith is the small price we pay to convert those shares of affliction into the windfall of glory.

By the way, that "eternal weight of glory" starts right now because eternity is timeless. Peace and joy in the Holy Spirit are a couple of those eternal riches available to us now. As we look through eyes of faith at the unseen things—seeing ourselves raised up with Christ and seated with him at the throne of glory—we truly reckon ourselves alive to God.

Surrender for Victory

One final issue remains: how to distinguish surrender to the purifying hand of God from passive acceptance of evil. Whenever pain of any kind comes, my advice is to push back against it and pray insistently yet humbly for relief. Our example is Paul who three times pled with the Lord to take away his "thorn in the flesh." Paul stopped praying only when the Lord said, "My grace is sufficient for you, for my power is made perfect in weakness" (2 Cor 12:7–9).

Having heard from the Lord, Paul then was content with his suffering (verse 10). Unlike resignation to evil, which has a bitter taste, contentment is the sweet fruit of godly surrender. We can identify the Father's discipline by the "peaceful fruit of righteousness" it yields (Heb 12:11).

Rather than resign ourselves to bondage of any kind, we realize that it is from godly surrender that we resist evil and that our authority over evil is in proportion to our submission to God. Sometimes God tests our heart to prove the genuineness of our faith and character (Rom 5:3–4). Other times he teaches us how to wage war. Along the way we resist the temptations to rebel, to envy, to be bitter, and instead fight from an attitude of praise and thanksgiving.

Soon after my conversion I began to sense my need for deliverance from the oppressive work of demons. God provided the help I needed through a chance encounter with a man who became my mentor, Clate Risley. I will say a little more about this deliverance in the next chapter.

We have victory through Jesus Christ (1 Cor 15:57). His bold proclamation became my heart's cry: "If the Son makes you free, you shall be free indeed" (John 8:36).

Because our Father always accomplishes his purpose and will do so in you as he is doing in me, I am confident that God is romancing you, converting you to a lover of him, and through trial shaping you into the image of his Son.

18

Chasing the God of Love

MOTORING IN MY WHEELCHAIR from one end of a mall to the other, I was thinking about several verses in Philippians 2 a few days before they would be the subject of my sermon. I was telling Jesus how great he is, marveling that he would leave heaven for earth and servanthood that would end with an excruciating death.

Passing one storefront after another I imagined his honor in heaven, and wondered how he could let go of such glory for the pain and shame of the cross.

Suddenly Jesus spoke to my spirit, "I let go of all this so I could grab hold of you." It was personal! He wanted me! The Lord of the entire universe came from heaven to be my friend. I studied the faces of those walking toward me, some bright and cheerful yet so many others, even the very young, with eyes searching for something to ease their pain. If only I could tell each one that God gave up his life of glory to grab hold of you and you and you.

Someone might dare to give up his or her life to rescue a good person, Paul says in Romans 5:7. In that case, none of us qualified for rescue by Jesus, because we were sinners and enemies of God. "But God demonstrates his own love toward us, in that while we were still sinners, Christ died for us" (verse 8 NASB).

Jesus took on himself your and my sin. He became "a curse for us," says Paul in Galatians 3:13. Here is proof, Martin Luther wrote, that Christ has for the sake of all people "become the greatest transgressor, murderer, adulterer, thief, rebel, blasphemer, etc., that ever was or could be in all the world."[1] He became sin for me.

"Though he was rich, yet for your sakes he became poor," says Paul in 2 Corinthians 8:9. Jesus tossed aside gold and diamonds to embrace my filthy rags.

This is the love of God, and it is offered to every human being. Paul prayed that you and I would know this love of Christ. It's wide, long, deep, and high: wide enough to reach the whole world, long enough to span eternity, high enough to raise us to heaven, and deep enough to rescue us from sin and Satan's grip (Eph 3:17–19).

Grateful for God's Goodness

I wrote this book out of gratitude to God for letting me find him. In reality, he found me and invited me into the reciprocal embrace of the family of God. Discovering his delight in me, I found my delight in him.

God will satisfy your soul as he has mine, so chase after him. Run to him especially when you think you have failed him, when shame and guilt knock at the door of your heart, and you will find his arms wide open.

Do what David suggests: taste God and you will see that he is good (Ps 34:8). Chase after him all the days of your life, my young friend, and you will find it to be the same for you. Your besetting sins are no problem for him to solve. Victory begins with thinking of yourself as he does: righteous and a new creation in Christ, dead to sin, a loved child of God. Reckon yourself so and go on the attack by the power of the Holy Spirit.

To encourage your own chasing after God, I will tell of a few times he has surprised me with his love and the refreshing of the Holy Spirit. These experiences have taught me that when we do

---

1. Luther, *Commentary*, 114.

seek God he delights to satisfy our hunger for him, and he surprises us with his love.

If there is a lesson I hope to convey through these memories, it is the importance of positioning ourselves for God to do his work in us. This means going where God is—seeking out people who can help us and gatherings where we can encounter the power and love of God. One encounter with God can accomplish more than years of counseling and therapy (not to say these have no value). Seek God where he may be found, and ask him to direct you.

Looking back, my biggest problem was not so much physical weakness but the crippling of my soul. Fear, shame, jealousy, and envy were some of the shackles on my heart. And I had given ground to the devil that had to be taken back. Here is a little more information on each of these strongholds.

Weak Body, Wounded Soul

I inherited a form of spinal muscular atrophy that causes a gradual weakening of muscles. The first symptom was my inability in the sixth grade to rise from a deep knee bend. By my late teens and early twenties, I was walking short distances by swinging my legs awkwardly to the side. I could climb stairs by leaning on a railing with my right arm and throwing my left leg up to the next step.

Attending the University of Oregon from 1962 to 1966, I was fearful of not being able to get up from chairs after classes. I had to sit either in a chair fixed to the floor or one in the last row with its back to the wall. To get up, I leaned with right hand on the back of chair while stretching my feet out in front, and I alternated my feet back an inch at a time until I could gain sufficient arch to be able to stand up. I wore Hush Puppies because their crepe soles stuck to the floor if they were wet. That meant I had to carry water in a small container and sprinkle it on the floor casually with no one watching. Or I would drop a raisin on the floor and squish it under my feet.

I was scared and ashamed to go through these awkward motions with anyone looking, and only my desire for an education overcame my embarrassment.

Chicago Deliverance

I mentioned at the end of the previous chapter my deliverance through the help of Clate Risley. It took place on the Wheaton College campus in August 1972, four years after I was saved. Clate introduced himself during a break in a spiritual life seminar I was attending with friends from our church. Clate took immediate interest in my weakness and asked about the cause. He invited my assistant Ron Woodruff and me to join him for lunch.

I told Clate about chronic insomnia that began soon after I committed to pray and seek God each day. I also mentioned I had in high school played with a Ouija board and participated in table-lifting séances. Clate right away discerned demonic involvement.

Clate put together a team and next evening led the session in a dormitory room. I don't recall details of the procedure other than that Clate and the team commanded several demons to leave. That night I slept well the first time in five months. Even more astonishing, the next day I was so full of joy on the flight back to Eugene I felt I could fly without the airplane![2]

For the next two years until his death Clate encouraged me with letters and phone calls, carving time out of a schedule that took him around the world. Clate was known as Mr. Sunday School of America because of his passion for Christian education and service in the National Association of Evangelicals as the executive secretary of the National Sunday School Association. When I met him, he was head of Worldwide Christian Education Ministries.

---

2. For more information on this topic, you may want to read Karl Payne's helpful book *Spiritual Warfare: Christians, Demonization and Deliverance* (WND Books, 2011). For inspiration in this battle, be sure to read *Waking the Dead* by John Eldredge (Thomas Nelson, 2006).

Clate taught me to understand my identity in Christ, to exercise my will against sin and Satan, to insist on victory from a position of humility before God, and to live a lifestyle of praising God. To avoid controversy, he said little on the public stage about spiritual warfare, acknowledging with a wink that some of his fellow Baptists were afraid of both the devil and the Holy Spirit.

The Vineyard

Christine and I heard of John Wimber and the Vineyard from Karsten Musaeus, a former member of our church who had moved to Los Angeles. Upon learning that John Wimber would hold a seminar in Houston at a church other friends[3] attended, we flew there in February 1984. The Spirit-filled worship and John Wimber's ministry of mercy, healing, and deliverance so touched our hearts that we wanted more.

After attending Vineyard seminars in Anaheim and Seattle, we invited teams from Anaheim to hold seminars at our church, including one led by Bob and Penny Fulton[4] that blessed many people. Soon we became the Eugene Vineyard Fellowship.

One infilling of the Spirit at a 1985 conference in Albany, Oregon, led by Brent Rue, Vineyard coordinator for our Northwest district, imparted a lasting confidence in the Father's love and affection for me. Wave after wave of Holy Spirit love flooded my soul for more than an hour, and I emerged from this cocoon of love only when a well-meaning friend during a break asked if I was okay.

God has surprised me on many other occasions, including renewal meetings, altar calls at church, and notably a workshop on the filling of the Holy Spirit taught by a team member of the Billy Graham Evangelistic Association at a pastor's conference in

---

3. Don and Carol Steele were also former members of our church and had served in deliverance ministry.

4. Bob was the Vineyard pastor in charge of the network of churches; Penny was John Wimber's sister-in-law.

Spokane, Washington.[5] The leader of this small assembly prayed for the Holy Spirit to fill everyone present, and the aftermath of this low-key event was for me intense, lasting joy.

Position Yourself for the Love of God

I share these experiences to encourage your own seeking of God. Position yourself by going where God is, whether your "prayer closet" or assemblies with other believers. God will shower you with his love and surprise you with joy, even when you feel least worthy and expect nothing more from God than to enjoy his presence, which alone is worth any price.

Go especially to God's word, which proclaims God is *for* us, no matter the circumstances of our life. Note the flawless logic of the Apostle Paul: "If God is for us, who can be against us? He who did not spare his own Son but gave him up for us all, how will he not also with him graciously give us all things?" (Rom 8:31–32). My friend, Paul assures you that nothing can separate you from the love of Christ. God wants to impart this assurance so deeply in your heart that you will never again doubt his love and affection for you.

Every human being seeks love, joy, and peace, the three most desired emotional states. The world promises these things but cannot deliver on its promise, because no product, achievement, fleshly indulgence, or refined work of art can ultimately satisfy this human craving.

The people of God are not promised freedom from tribulation, distress, persecution, famine, nakedness, peril, or sword. We are promised that God is for us in the midst of these things. Even at the worst of times, we can be assured of Christ's love. And Paul in Romans 8:31–39 is not talking about merely an abstract concept of love. *We can know and feel God's love.* It penetrates our entire being—spirit, mind, heart, emotions.

---

5. I am grateful to Bob Agnew, who went on to become Salem Radio Network news anchor, for his help during this trip.

Emotions Follow Truth

How do we enter into the love that settles in our heart and yields an abiding sense of peace and joy? This is how I answer: God changes our emotions as we devote our minds to the truth of God's word and do what it says.

We know where love, joy, and peace come from; they are fruit of the Spirit. That is why only God can fundamentally change our emotions, and he does it as we seek and obey him. As Jesus said, "If you keep my commandments, you will abide in my love, just as I have kept my Father's commandments and abide in his love. These things I have spoken to you, that my joy may be in you, and that your joy may be full" (John 15:10–11).

Paul put it this way: "What you have learned and received and heard and seen in me—practice these things, and the God of peace will be with you" (Phil 4:9).

We stand on the truth that God is for us whether we feel it or not, knowing that feelings will follow fact and faith. Reckon yourself alive to his love and love him by obeying him. He promises to fill you with his joy.

A worthy spiritual exercise is to meditate on Romans 8:31–39 and make your stand, reckoning that what Paul says about you is true, because they are God's word for you. Hide these truths in your mind and heart and turn them into prayer as you seek God to make them real in your life. I think you will begin to believe and feel God's affection for you and his peace in you.

Summary

A Model for Reckoning

FIVE ACTION STEPS SUMMARIZE the central truths of the preceding chapters into a five-part model for reckoning ourselves dead to sin and alive to God in Christ (Rom 6:11). There is nothing original about these five thought processes and actions, which appear frequently in the New Testament as responsibilities of believers. The model's value comes from taking these steps in the context of reckoning.

Reckoning is thinking that aligns with God's thoughts. We recognize what God says is true and see ourselves as God does—righteous in Christ and therefore dead to sin and alive to God. Wherever you start in your sanctification process, no matter how far from God's declared truth your practice of that truth is, this model's five steps can help you narrow the gap

The steps are arranged in somewhat of a logical order, but you can put them to use in any order you find helpful.

1. Renew your mind

To think of yourself as God does, you must read what he says about you. Make Bible reading a habit and ask God to open your eyes to its truth, particularly what Christ accomplished on your behalf through his death and resurrection. Read, memorize, and contemplate what the Bible says about the identity of believers in Christ as described in chapter 4. You must learn to think of yourself as possessing all the blessings that come with being united with Christ.

Your imagination performs an essential role in reckoning because you must see beyond your circumstances and present behavior to a new realm of freedom. Imagination is a powerful tool for evil or for good. You can use it to lust or to meditate on things that are noble, just, pure, lovely, good, virtuous, and praiseworthy (Phil 4:8). What does it look like to be sitting above with Christ at the right hand of God (Col 3:1–3)?

Sanctify your imagination: set it apart for service to God. Then, if your problem is lust, use your imagination to meditate on Psalm 1 and 1 Thessalonians 4:1–8. Set your mind on the things of the Spirit (Rom 8:5) by meditating on Ephesians 5:18–21 and Galatians 5:13–26. Select a Psalm, such as 16, 25, 27, 34, 36, 37, 40, 91, 103, or 116, and personalize it into a prayer. Declare over yourself the Bible verses collected in the Appendix.

2. Repent

Repentance is a change of mind and affections by which you turn away not just from sin but also from worldly mindsets and false conceptions of yourself and of God. Making this mental change requires faith. You must trust God sufficiently to give up old, familiar habits and ways of thinking for a new lifestyle that may seem quite foreign to you.

To repent of sin, start with confession: tell God what he already knows about your sins. Commit to doing right and give up your right to do wrong. Unless you hate your sin and want to give it up, these steps will avail you little. You can turn from sin with confidence that it no longer holds you captive and turn to God with assurance that he accepts and cherishes you.

3. Request the Spirit's help

Biblical reckoning is a positive activity you approach with confidence, because you are counting on what God has already accomplished for you. Yes, it takes effort, but you already have the victory. Focus foremost not on your sin and failures but on your Helper the Spirit. Walk by the Spirit, as Paul commands, and you will not carry out the deeds of the flesh (Gal 5:16). The payoff is that you will find the things of the Spirit so enjoyable that you will naturally lose interest in the things of the flesh.

Ask the Father now to give you a fresh filling of the Holy Spirit (see Luke 11:13). Invite the Holy Spirit to fill you, immerse you, empower you. As you engage in activities the Bible identifies as empowered by the Spirit, you will release the Spirit's power in your life. These include worship, thanksgiving, humble service to others, giving to the needy, prayer, Bible reading and meditation, and participation in a church that honors Jesus Christ.

4. Resist sin and the devil

At this point you move from reckoning to active obedience: "Therefore do not let sin reign in your mortal body, that you should obey it in its lusts" (Rom 6:12 NKJ). You refuse to live contrary to your identity in Christ. This is no time for passivity. Be ruthless against sin lest it dominate you once again. If your old self tries to rise from the grave, push it back in the coffin. Enforce the word of God in your life. Stand firm against the devil in the strength of the Lord, and rebuke demonic lies and temptations. There is power in the name: *Jesus Christ!*

5. Command

Your tongue has the power to bring death or life (Prov 18:21). Preach to yourself words that comfort and encourage (Prov 16:24). Psalm 119 is a good model for godly assertions: "I will praise . . . ," "I will seek . . . ," "I will meditate on . . . ," and "I will delight in . . . ." Command the mountain of unforgiveness and bitterness to flee (Mark 11:22–24). Proclaim out loud against any other stronghold of sin: "I am dead to lust!" "I am dead to anger!"

There you have it, four Rs and a C for ease of memory (4RC): Renew, Repent, Request, Resist, and Command. We could add a fifth R for Reckoning but that is not necessary because all of these steps together constitute a practical method for obeying Paul's command.

Keep doing any or all of these steps as needed, and do not give up. Be patient and try not to compare your progress with that of others. You will reap in due time, so keep sowing good seed. Trust and wait on God.

Your work in the sanctification process will become easier as you take your mind off yourself and make pleasing God your goal. *He* is your reward. Your heavenly Father and your Redeemer are passionate to make you a suitable, holy bride and a child exhibiting the character of the family of God. Make their passion yours. Catch it, live it, and pass it on to others.

Conclusion

The Book That Reads Me

A S AUTHOR OF THIS book I have the right to identify its main character. On the basis of all the Bible verses cited and their ability to transform both Cody and me, it's obvious the lead role is played by the word of God.

I am in awe of the power of Scripture—illuminated and applied to mind and heart by the Holy Spirit—to transform troubled youth into confident lovers of God. Cody did not, and neither did I, envision at the beginning of our walks with Jesus Christ how great a love the Lord would have for all of his young volunteers to take us on this journey of faith and freedom.

In addition to this book's theme verse, Romans 6:11, several other passages had transformative power in my growth as a Christian. In my late twenties, as I wrote in chapter 17, I learned to view affliction with the eyes of faith through my study of the Vinedresser's pruning in John 15 and the unseen things in 2 Corinthians 4. Shortly thereafter, I encountered the self-giving love of God in Hebrews 2:10. All four of these passages came alive to me in study and meditation, as I dug deep in particular verses when the Spirit seemed to say there is more here to learn.

Other passages that contributed to my growth are Ephesians 1, Colossians 3, Galatians 5, Psalm 110, and Psalm 119, especially the verse I often prayed: "Open my eyes, that I may behold wonderful things from your law" (18, NASB). What passages have had greatest influence on you?

As we seek to close the gap between our position of declared righteousness and our practice of that righteousness, the Bible is our trainer and the Holy Spirit is our guide.

I took to regular reading of the Bible immediately after being saved and soon realized that as I was reading through the Bible the Bible was reading me.

In John 15, right after Jesus told the disciples his Father prunes every branch that it may bear more fruit, he says this in verse 3: "You are already clean because of the word which I have spoken to you." Merrill C. Tenney explains the word's cleansing power:

> The means by which pruning or cleaning is done is the Word of God. It condemns sin; it inspires holiness; it promotes growth. As Jesus applied the words God gave him to the lives of the disciples, they underwent a pruning process that removed evil from them and conditioned them for further service.[1]

Paul says in Ephesians 5:26 that Christ is cleansing his bride the church by washing her with water through the word. The word of God can do this cleansing work because it is alive with divine power. It peers into my inner world and discerns the thoughts and intentions of my heart (Heb 4:12).

The word derives these abilities from its Author, who "breathed" it into existence and made it profitable for training in righteousness (2 Tim 3:16).

Knowing God's word is both authoritative and reliable, we have confidence to apply what it says about Christ's death and resurrection and about our position in him.

The most important lesson of this book is to make Bible reading and study your own passion so it will do its work in you. At the same time, pray for the Holy Spirit's illumination of Scripture to your mind and heart. Paul's prayers for the Ephesians in chapters

---

1. Tenney, "John," 151.

1 and 3 are excellent patterns for asking that the eyes of your heart be opened to the truth and majesty of God through his revelation of himself.

I began this study with the question posed by the author of Psalm 119 in verse 9: "How can a young man keep his way pure?" His answer—by guarding his way according to God's word—applies even more today, now that God has more fully revealed himself in the gospel of Jesus Christ. So let us do as that man did and store up the word in our hearts that we might not sin against God (verse 11). Above all, may we adore the Word who became flesh and died to make us alive, today.

Appendix

Scriptural Declarations
of Freedom in Christ

A LL SCRIPTURE IS INSPIRED by God and profitable for training in righteousness (2 Tim 3:16). The Bible verses compiled and personalized here are especially potent for training your mind and heart to believe that Jesus Christ has done everything necessary to set you free from sin and help you come alive to God. Some are proclamations and others are prayerful requests.

For best results, proclaim these scriptural truths out loud over yourself daily. Their arrangement in three groups allows for use in a three-day cycle. Declaring these words will enforce in your life the truth that sets you free (see John 8:30–36).

Day 1

Hear, O LORD, and be merciful to me! O LORD, be my helper (Ps 30:10)!

Please lead me in your truth and teach me, for you are the God of my salvation; for you I wait all the day long (Ps 25:5).

I acknowledged my sin to you, and I did not cover my iniquity; I said, "I will confess my transgressions to the LORD," and you forgave the iniquity of my sin (Ps 32:5).

If I say I have no sin, I deceive myself, and the truth is not in me. If I confess my sins, he is faithful and just to forgive me of my sins and to cleanse me from all unrighteousness (1 John 1:8–9).

If I sin, I have an advocate with the Father, Jesus Christ the righteous. He is the propitiation for my sins, and not for mine only but also for the sins of the whole world (1 John 2:1–2).

I was dead in my trespasses, but God made me alive together with Christ, having forgiven me all my trespasses (Col 2:13).

With my whole heart I seek you, Father; let me not wander from your commandments! I have stored up your word in my heart, that I might not sin against you (Ps 119:10–11).

I do not have a righteousness of my own that comes from the law, but that which comes through faith in Christ, the righteousness from God that depends on faith (Phil 3:9).

I put to death what is earthly in me: sexual immorality, impurity, passion, evil desire, and covetousness, which is idolatry (Col 3:5).

My soul clings to the dust; give me life according to your word (Ps 119:25)!

God the Father chose me in Christ before the foundation of the world, that I should be holy and blameless. In love he predestined me for adoption as a son through Jesus Christ, according to the purpose of his will and to the praise of his glorious grace (Eph 1:4–6).

He restores my soul. He leads me in paths of righteousness for his name's sake (Ps 23:3).

One thing have I asked of the LORD, that will I seek after: that I may dwell in the house of the Lord all the days of my life, to gaze upon the beauty of the Lord and to inquire in his temple (Ps 27:4).

I have been justified by faith and I have peace with God through my Lord Jesus Christ (Rom 5:1).

I have been raised with Christ, so I seek the things that are above, where Christ is, seated at the right hand of God. I set my mind on things that are above, not on things that are on earth, for I have died, and my life is hidden with Christ in God (Col 3:1–3).

By this I know that I have come to know him, if I keep his commandments (1 John 2:3).

Why are you cast down, O my soul, and why are you in turmoil within me? Hope in God; for I shall again praise him, my salvation and my God (Ps 42:5–6).

I was baptized with Christ into his death and burial and then was raised from the dead with him so I can now walk in newness of life (Rom 6:3–4).

My old sin nature was crucified with Christ so that I am no longer a slave of sin. I have been set free from sin and now live with Christ (Rom 6:6–8, 18, 22).

Heavenly Father, fill me anew with the Holy Spirit (Luke 11:13, Eph 5:18).

The Son has set me free, and I will be free indeed (John 8:36)!

Day 2

I reckon myself dead to sin and alive to God in Christ Jesus (Rom 6:11).

I refuse to allow sin to rule over me to make me obey its passions (Rom 6:12).

I put away all malice, deceit, hypocrisy, envy, and slander. Like a newborn infant, I long for the pure spiritual milk, that by it I may grow up into salvation—for I have tasted that the Lord is good (1 Pet 2:1–3).

God raised me from the dead and gave me new life, so I surrender and yield every part of my being (mind, will, heart, and all parts of my body) to God for living righteously (Rom 6:13).

God adopted me into his family and I am now a fellow heir with Christ. The Spirit leads me and teaches me that I am God's child (Rom 8:14–17).

God is *for* me and nothing can separate me from his love. Since the Father already gave up his precious Son for me, I can trust that he will give me all good things (Rom 8:31–39).

Keep me as the apple of your eye, and hide me in the shadow of your wings (Ps 17:8).

Keep back your servant also from presumptuous sins; let them not have dominion over me (Ps 19:13)!

Let the words of my mouth and the meditation of my heart be acceptable in your sight (Ps 19:14).

Deal bountifully with your servant, that I may live and keep your word (Ps 119:17).

I have chosen the way of faithfulness; I set your rules before me. I cling to your testimonies, O LORD; let me not be put to shame (Ps 119:30–31)!

I put away all anger, wrath, malice, slander, and obscene talk from my mouth. I do not lie to others, seeing that I have put off the old self with its practices and have put on the new self, which is being renewed in knowledge after the image of its creator (Col 3:8–10).

Lord, please turn my eyes from looking at worthless things; and give me life in your ways. Behold, I long for your precepts; in your righteousness give me life (Ps 119:37, 40)!

Before I was afflicted I went astray, but now I keep your word. You are good and do good; teach me your statutes (Ps 119:67–68).

Through your precepts I get understanding; therefore I hate every false way (Ps 119:104).

The Father has delivered me from the domain of darkness and transferred me to the kingdom of his beloved Son, in whom I have redemption, the forgiveness of my sins (Col 1:13–14).

By grace I have been saved through faith. And this is not my own doing; it is the gift of God, not a result of works, so that I may not boast (Eph 2:8–9).

I no longer have to obey the law of sin and death, for I have been set free in Christ Jesus by the law of the Spirit of life (Rom 8:2).

As God's chosen one, holy and beloved, I put on a compassionate heart, kindness, humility, meekness, and patience. If I have a complaint against anyone, I forgive that person as the Lord has forgiven me. And above all these I put on love (Col 3:12–14).

Heavenly father, fill me anew with the Holy Spirit (Luke 11:13, Eph 5:18).

The Son has set me free, and I will be free indeed (John 8:36)!

Day 3

Teach me your way, O LORD, that I may walk in your truth; please unite my heart to fear your name (Ps 86:11).

In Christ I have redemption through his blood, the forgiveness of my trespasses, according to the riches of his grace (Eph 1:7).

God gave me a spirit not of fear but of power and love and self-control (2 Tim 1:7–8).

I submit myself to God. I resist the devil, and he will flee from me. I draw near to God, and he will draw near to me (Jas 4:7–8).

I pray that the God of my Lord Jesus Christ, the Father of glory, may give me the Spirit of wisdom and of revelation in the knowledge of him, so the eyes of my heart will be enlightened and I may know what is the hope to which he has called me (Eph 1:17–18).

God, who is rich in mercy, because of the great love with which he loved me, even when I was dead in my trespasses, made me alive together with Christ—by grace I have been saved—and raised me up with him and seated me with him in the heavenly places in Christ Jesus (Eph 2:4–6).

I live according to the Spirit so I no longer set my mind on the things of the flesh, but I set my mind on the things of the Spirit, where I find life and peace (Rom 8:5–6).

I put off my old self, which belongs to my former manner of life and is corrupt through deceitful desires, and I put on the new self, created after the likeness of God in true righteousness and holiness (Eph: 4:22–24).

I am strong in the Lord and in the strength of his might. I put on the whole armor of God, that I may be able to stand against the schemes of the devil (Eph 6:10–11).

I fasten on the belt of truth, I put on the breastplate of righteousness, and as shoes for my feet I put on the readiness given by the gospel of peace. In all circumstances I take up the shield of faith, with which I can extinguish all the flaming darts of the evil one; and I take the helmet of salvation, and the sword of the Spirit, which is the word of God, praying at all times in the Spirit (Eph 6:14–18).

My soul yearns for God in the night; my spirit within me earnestly seeks God (Isa 26:9).

I am not anxious about anything, but in everything by prayer and supplication with thanksgiving I let my requests be made known to God. And the peace of God, which surpasses all understanding, will guard my heart and my mind in Christ Jesus (Phil 4:6–7).

The will of God is my sanctification: that I abstain from sexual immorality; that I know how to control my own body in holiness and honor, not in the passion of lust, and that I not transgress and wrong my brother or sister in this matter, because the Lord is an avenger in all these things. For God has not called me for impurity, but in holiness (1 Thess 4:3–7).

I have tasted and seen that the LORD is good (Ps 34:8)!

I delight to do your will, O my God; your law is within my heart (Ps 40:8).

See what kind of love the Father has given me, that I should be called a child of God. I know that when he appears I shall be like him, because I shall see him as he is. And everyone who thus hopes in him purifies himself as he is pure (1 John 3:1–3).

I delight myself in the LORD, and I know he will give me the desires of my heart (Ps 37:4).

The LORD my God is in my midst, a mighty one who will save; he will rejoice over me with gladness; he will quiet me by his love; he will exult over me with loud singing (Zeph 3:17).

I will walk by the Spirit so I will not gratify the deeds of the flesh (Gal 5:16).

The Son has set me free, and I will be free indeed (John 8:36)!

Afterthought

The Father's Smile and Blessing

A S MOTIVATION TO SURRENDER our lives to God and live in obedience to him, nothing matches our experience of the Father's love. What is his countenance toward you, my friend? You may think the Father looks at you with a frown, but I want you to see his welcoming smile.

No matter what you have done, if you come to him with a repentant heart he will greet you with not only a smile but also a hug and a kiss. The only time in Scripture we see the Father in a hurry is when he runs out to greet and embrace his returning prodigal son (Luke 15:20). Jesus told that story to portray the forgiving and loving heart of our heavenly Father.

So his people would know that his intention is for their good, God gave Moses a new command that became known as The Aaronic Blessing. He told Moses to speak to the priests—Aaron and his sons—and tell them to bless the people of Israel. God also gave Moses the words the priests must proclaim over the people.

In the new covenant all believers are priests (1 Pet 2:9), and we have been called to inherit the blessing (1 Pet 3:9). So I am authorized to bless you as Aaron and his sons did on God's people of their day, and you in turn can bless others. We see in the last line of this blessing that it is God who blesses and we are his instruments.

My friend, as you read the blessing on the next page, understand that God is speaking directly to you, from his heart to yours. Know that God intends to bless you. He wants you to see his smile of acceptance and to experience his grace and peace.

The Aaronic Blessing

The LORD bless you and keep you;
The LORD make his face to shine upon you
and be gracious to you;
The LORD lift up his countenance upon you
and give you peace.
So shall they put my name upon the people of
Israel, and I will bless them.

(NUM 6:24–27)

Bibliography

Arndt, William F., and F. Wilbur Gingrich. *A Greek-English Lexicon of the New Testament and Other Early Christian Literature*. Chicago: The University of Chicago Press, 1957.

Brunner, Emil. "The Christian Understanding of Man." In *The Christian Understanding of Man*, edited by T. E. Jessop. New York: Willett, Clark and Co., 1938. http://discovertheword.org/?p=1618.

Einstein, Albert. *Science, Philosophy and Religion, A Symposium*. New York: Conference on Science, Philosophy and Religion in Their Relation to the Democratic Way of Life, Inc., 1941. http://einsteinandreligion.com/scienceandreligion2.html.

Eldredge, John. *Waking the Dead: The Glory of a Heart Fully Alive*. Nashville, TN: Thomas Nelson, 2006.

Fromke, DeVern. *The Ultimate Intention*. Cloverdale, IL: Sure Foundation, 1974.

Groothuis, Douglas. *Christian Apologetics: A Comprehensive Case for Biblical Faith*. Downers Grove, IL: InterVarsity, 2011.

Grudem, Wayne A. *Systematic Theology: an Introduction to Biblical Doctrine*. Grand Rapids: Zondervan, 2004. Logos edition.

Harrison, Everett F. "Romans." In *The Expositor's Bible Commentary, Volume 10: Romans through Galatians,* edited by F. E. Gaebelein, 85–101. Grand Rapids: Zondervan, 1976. Logos edition.

Kruse, Colin G. *Paul's Letter to the Romans*. The Pillar New Testament Commentary, edited by D. A. Carson. Grand Rapids: Eerdmans, 2012. Logos edition.

Leaf, Caroline. *Switch On Your Brain: The Key to Peak Happiness, Thinking, and Health*. Grand Rapids: Baker, 2013.

Longenecker, Richard N. *The Epistle to the Romans: A Commentary on the Greek Text*. The New International Greek Testament Commentary, edited by I. Howard Marshall and Donald A. Hagner. Grand Rapids: Eerdmans, 2016.

Luther, Martin. *Commentary on St. Paul's Epistle to the Galatians*. Christian Classics Ethereal Library. Original edition, 1535. http://www.ccel.org/ ccel/luther/galatians.vi.html.

Molinos, Michael. "Two Spiritual Experiences." In *100 Days in the Secret Place*, by Gene Edwards. Shippensburg, PA: Destiny Image, 2001. Kindle edition.

Moo, Douglas J. *The Epistle to the Romans*. The New International Commentary on the New Testament, edited by Gordon D. Fee. Grand Rapids: Eerdmans, 1996. Logos edition.

Moreland, J. P. *Kingdom Triangle: Recover the Christian Mind, Renovate the Soul, Restore the Spirit's Power*. Grand Rapids: Zondervan, 2007.

Noonan, Peggy. "What We Have Learned." *The Wall Street Journal* (November 23, 2001). http://www.wsj.com/articles/SB1006475266288749840.

Packer, J. I. *Concise Theology: A Guide to Historic Christian Beliefs*. Wheaton, IL: Tyndale, 1993. Logos edition.

————. "John Owen Put Me Straight." *Christian History* 89: Richard Baxter and the English Puritans, 2006. https://www.christianhistoryinstitute.org/ magazine/article/john-owen-put-me-straight/.

Payne, Karl I. *Spiritual Warfare: Christians, Demonization and Deliverance*. Washington DC: WND Books, 2011. Kindle edition.

Piper, John. *Desiring God: Meditations of a Christian Hedonist*. Sisters, OR: Multnomah, 2003.

Simmons, Geoffrey, M.D. *What Darwin Didn't Know: A Doctor Dissects the Theory of Evolution*. Eugene, OR: Harvest House, 2004.

————. *Billions of Missing Links: A Rational Look at the Mysteries Evolution Can't Explain*. Eugene, OR: Harvest House, 2007.

Sproul, R. C. (1994). *The Gospel of God: An Exposition of Romans*. Great Britain: Christian Focus, 1994. Logos edition.

Tan, Paul Lee. *Encyclopedia of 7700 Illustrations: Signs of the Times*. Garland, TX: Bible Communications, 1996.

Tenney, Merrill C. "John." In *The Expositor's Bible Commentary, Volume 9: John and Acts*, edited by F. E. Gaebelein. Grand Rapids: Zondervan, 1981. Logos edition.

Warfield, B.B. *On the Emotional Life of Our Lord*. In *Biblical and Theological Studies: A Commemoration of 100 Years of Princeton Seminary*, 35–90. New York: Charles Scribner's Sons, 1912. https://www.monergism.com/ emotional-life-our-lord.

Witherington, Ben, III. *New Testament Rhetoric: An Introductory Guide to the Art of Persuasion in and of the New Testament*. Eugene, OR: Cascade, 2009. Logos edition.

Wolfe, Alan. "The Pursuit of Autonomy." *The New York Times Magazine* (May 7, 2000). http://www.nytimes.com/2000/05/07/magazine/the-pursuit-of-autonomy.html?pagewanted=all.